When a Father Leaves

By Ann Evelyn

WHEN A FATHER LEAVES

Copyright © 2016 by Ann Evelyn

ISBN: 978-0-9934910-2-3
eISBN: 978-0-9934910-3-0

All rights reserved.

No part of this publication may be reproduced, stored in a retrieval system, or transmitted in any form or by any means, electronic, mechanical, photocopying or otherwise, without prior written consent of the publisher except as provided by under United Kingdom copyright law. Short extracts may be used for review purposes with credits given.

Published by
Maurice Wylie Media
Bethel Media House
Tobermore
Magherafelt,
Northern Ireland
BT45 5SG (UK)

www.MauriceWylieMedia.com

INSPIRATIONAL CHRISTIAN PUBLISHER

Create | Brand | Establish

Dedication

In memory of my gentle Mother who was full of kindness and love. I think of her as being gentle, for she spoke in a soft voice and people who knew her would say that I am very like her in my manner, attitudes and looks. I know, had I walked in her shoes, I would probably have taken the same steps she took. Although our time together was short, I am grateful that I got to know her and will always remember her fondly.

I thank God for the gift of life and love. Without Him I am nothing.

With thanks to my husband John who loves me for the person I am. Thank you for your love and care every day and for your encouragement and understanding.

To my friends who have shared and helped me on my life's journey. Two-legged and four-legged ones. Rover, you will always have a special place in my heart. You are the first dog I ever loved and you were there for me when no one else was. Sorry I wet your fur with my tears so many times.

Chapters

	INTRODUCTION	7
1	**HUMBLE BEGINNINGS**	9
	Farewell Granny Alice	
2	**BLOWING IN THE WIND**	13
	On his best behaviour	
	Christmas cheer	
3	**BOMBING WHISKEY FACTORIES**	17
	Sundays at the pub	
	Dead in a ditch	
4	**MY PLAN**	21
	The same storm just a different day	
5	**MY MOTHER**	27
	School life	
	Odd one out	
	Changing my name	
6	**CRUEL TIMES**	31
	The weight of humiliation	
7	**FARM LIFE**	35
	Returning home	
	The Vintage Festival	
8	**MY FAITHFUL ROVER**	41
	Protection and hope	
9	**WATERING IT DOWN**	47
	Stranger in the dark	
	Boy trouble	
10	**MY HUSBAND**	53
	Gone forever	
	Our wedding day	
11	**MARRIED LIFE**	59
	The loss of my inheritance	
	My promised savings	

12	**THE GOLDEN POISON**	63
	None of my business	
13	**THE REAL TRUTH**	67
	Nowhere to call home	
	Time for healing	
14	**RESCUING UNCLE JAMES**	73
	Time for change	
15	**FAMILY TROUBLES**	79
	My final visit home	
16	**MY FADING FATHER**	83
	No job too small	
17	**OPENING UP ABOUT THE PAST**	87
	A dangerous lifestyle	
18	**PROBLEM PAGES**	93
	My Dad's lifetime of drink still haunts us	
	My drunken Dad will ruin our Christmas again	
	Father's rules	
19	**REUNITING THE BROTHERS**	99
	The matron's office	
20	**GETTING HIS OWN WAY**	103
21	**A COASTAL HOME**	107
	Father strikes again	
22	**LIFE WAS GOOD**	113
	Bad neighbours	
	Same old problems	
23	**A SAD TURN OF EVENTS**	117
	Goodbye Uncle James	
	Excluded once again	
24	**EXECUTOR ISSUES**	123
	All my own fault	
25	**TOTAL DEPENDENCE**	127
	More family problems	
	Goodbye Uncle David	
26	**LOVE AND RESPECT IS PRICELESS**	133
	Gone for good	
	A family wedding	
	Surgery to correct my painful past	
27	**FINAL THOUGHTS**	143

Introduction

Writing a book is something I thought I would never do. As a child I was always told by my father not to carry stories and to keep my mouth shut. Out of fear, I obeyed. But now I share my story not as a victim of a dysfunctional family, but as a survivor, in the hope that it will be a help to others living in a hard place. In life we cannot choose the family we are born into but we can choose not to be like them.

My family was caught up in the rot and dysfunction of alcoholism, but we can learn from others not to make the same mistakes and take responsibility for our own lives. We can make life better and make wiser choices.

I live in Ireland where abuse in the home and church has come to the public arena over the last number of years. It has rocked our world. The lies, the cover ups, the destruction of young peoples' lives in a place where they were supposed to be safe and cared for instead was rotten to the core. A lot of these people have carried the pain of this into adulthood and many have been unable to face life any longer. A childhood lasts a lifetime and abuse in any form against a child or adult is so wrong.

Over the years I have met many people who suffer from depression and mental health problems. Some of these people have shared their past with me. All of them have endured abuse from the family unit that was there to protect and care for them.

Psychologist Abraham Maslow talks about a hierarchy of needs.

In this he explains how the most basic human needs should to be met in our younger years for us to progress to be the best we can be. If these are not met it can cause many problems. I am not a medical expert but I wonder has this anything to do with the amount of mental health problems in our society? I have vast experience of alcohol abuse and know it can tear lives and families apart. Yet it is commonplace in our society to drink on a regular basis. In many countries the pub is a meeting place for family functions such as weddings, christenings, funerals, and birthdays. These same events have became in many instances a launch pad for a young life being drawn into alcoholism.

There is so much to enjoy in this life, so why would I want to throw that away to follow the crowd? Why make the choice to drink, smoke or do drugs when all it does is destroy lives? There is no benefit. It results in a multitude of problems, from broken homes, money problems, to wasted hours. I thank God every day that I have been strong enough to make the choice that my life would be different.

We get one life on this earth and I want to be the best I can be. Sometimes we go through life making judgements against others which is totally wrong. Often what goes on behind closed doors can be a very different story to what we see with our eyes, as my story will tell. I hope my story will be of help to others. Names and dates have been changed.

Chapter One

Humble Beginnings

The earliest memory of my childhood was living in the countryside with my brother Michael, our father, uncles James and David, and their mother Alice. We lived in a large Georgian mansion which was very run down. It looked beautiful on the outside but it was very cold inside and the facilities were outdated.

I remember Granny Alice being a very hard, cold woman in heart. She was not very tall and the years had taken their toll on her body. Her spine was curved and she always talked about her aches and pains. I never recall her showing love or care towards me or my brother Michael. Was she a product of her own upbringing? Was she treated the same in her family and knew no better? I didn't know, but what was very clear to me, was that my father was her golden boy. He could do no wrong in her eyes and in later years it made sense to me.

It all began in the mid-fifties when my parents got married in a small town in Ireland. My father was the youngest of three brothers and he had one sister. He was a big social drinker and was known as being the 'life and soul' of the party. My mother was the daughter of a shopkeeper and had one sister. When she met my father, I am sure she was aware that he drank quite a bit, but was probably taken in by his wit and charm, of which he had plenty.

After their wedding they moved into a house over a shop premises which was lovingly given to them by my grandfather, who had worked hard all his life farming. The family estate that we later lived on was being left to my eldest uncle but my grandfather managed to borrow the money to buy also the shop for my parents to give them a good start in life.

My grandfather knew my father had a problem with alcohol, but probably felt now that he was getting married, he would settle down and take responsibility for his wife and any children that would come along.

My brother Michael was born in 1958 and I was born in 1961. It did not take long for problems to appear in my parents marriage. Unfortunately, this new family home gave my father easy access to alcohol as there was a small pub at the back of the shop. My father was drinking heavily and bills were not being paid. Life was not easy for my mother Annette. My grandad helped to pay the bills, but he could only do so much. My father was still drinking and not taking any responsibility for sorting out his own life. Things deteriorated so he moved back to his mother on the farm, taking us with him.

I remember living in that big Georgian house without my mother around. To me as a child, that was the way life was. If I mentioned her name, it was always met with a silent reaction, or I was told not to ask questions and to mind my own business. As a child I learned it was easier not to speak of her.

Farewell Granny Alice...
My uncles James and David were quiet men, getting on with their lives, running the farms their father had left them following his death. He had split the estate in two and gave them a farm each, my father's inheritance was the shop and house that he still owned but no longer lived in. The farms created full-time work for everyone as there were plenty of sheep and cattle to tend to.

As my father wasn't interested in farm work, he took on the running of the finances and he would visit the town every week to do all our shopping as my uncles very rarely left the farm. Unfortunately after doing so, father would often return very drunk, I learned to stay out of his way when he'd been drinking. Arguments would then often erupt in the house because of this but my granny would always defend him.

My granny passed away when I was eight years old. I remember the night she died really vividly. She had been unwell for weeks, then prior to her passing, all the family were called. My brother Michael and I were sent to bed early, but I heard voices and footsteps on the wooden stairs several times during the night.

I lay in bed wondering what was going on. I could hear the distant chatter of voices and then I heard three knocks on my bedroom door so I got up. The door creaked as I gently opened it. The hallway was dimly lit by the light coming from the half-open door of my granny's room but no one was there. I got back into bed and covered my head with the warm blankets and wondered what tomorrow would bring.

The next morning I was told my granny had died during the night. I asked who knocked on my bedroom door to be told that it was nobody - that it was simply my imagination. A cold shiver ran down my spine. I knew I wasn't imagining it.

The funeral was held a few days later. Neighbours called to the house to extend their sympathy and my father busied himself, offering them tea and alcohol.

I tried to distance myself from it all, wondering what life would be like now that I was the only girl in the house. I was sad she was gone and stood with tears streaming down my face at her graveside. This made my brother and father cross and they warned me to pull myself together and not make a show of myself. As her coffin was lowered into the grave, I prayed to God to keep me strong to face the days that lay ahead.

Chapter Two

Blowing in the Wind

I have very few memories of my Granny Alice. She was a little grey-haired woman, always pottering about the house, doing her chores. She wore a wrap-over apron over her clothes. Her small frame was very frail and she was slightly bent over. She used to make bread and cook it in the large Aga cooker in the kitchen.

For the Aga to work properly the wind had to be blowing in the right direction, so that the draft on the chimney would keep the temperature correct to cook the dough. I remember her going to the back door to see what direction the trees were blowing in the wind. That was the deciding factor in whether or not the bread would be baked that day.

Once a week, she would take an old tin from the dresser in the kitchen. From this tin, she would take a bag of crisps and cut them in half with the scissors. She would give one half to my brother, and one half to me. It was the only act of kindness I remember from her.

Sadly, she lost a child very young, a little girl. She had also lost her husband and her body was crippled with pains and aches. Was this the reason I remember her as a hard, cold lady? Had life made her hard? Like me, maybe she didn't have any respect or love shown to her by her family. I know it's very hard to give what you don't receive, and I don't think she knew any different.

I remember her watching me one day leaving the house in a hurry, as an awful argument erupted between my father and uncles. I just had to get out as sometimes they were so bad, I was afraid someone would be hurt. I went to a neighbour who lived further down the road. He was an elderly man and always spoke kindly to me. I didn't mention the awful fight I had just ran away from, as my father had always warned me not to tell.

I remember it was a lovely, balmy summer evening. The trees around the farmyard were swaying in the breeze. The evening sun glistened through the moving branches. Despite the agony I was in, it was so peaceful. I wondered what fate would face me on my return home, but for the moment I was happy. I was sure I wouldn't even be missed. The hours passed and we chatted away together as he did his yard jobs.

As the evening was closing in, I heard the yard gate opening and saw my father making an entrance. He closed the gate and came over to where we were. I was frightened. He told me it was time to come home, made some small talk with the man I was with, and we left.

I had left the house and hadn't told anyone where I was going. Truth was, I didn't know where I was going, I only knew I had to get away. I walked the short distance home with my father. On entering the long, winding avenue up to the house I wondered what was going to happen. The avenue was steep and trees lined part of it, closer to the house. They hung over the path and cast evening shadows over us and all the while, my father never uttered a word.

He was maybe angry at himself for causing the argument, that caused me to leave the way I did. Somewhere deep inside his soul, he must know the main reason for the disharmony in our home, was his fault. My father opened the back door and I walked in ahead of him, without a word. I felt it was best to say nothing in case an argument erupted again.

The light was off in the kitchen but I could see my granny

standing at the cooker. She was cross and told my father I should be punished. I stayed silent and walked through the kitchen up to my bedroom. I thanked God I was home safe, went to bed and wondered what tomorrow would bring.

On his best behaviour...
Before granny died, her sister used to visit in the summer time. She was a lovely lady, and always had a gift for us when she came. She worked in Dublin as a housekeeper for a family. I always brought her a cup of tea in the mornings while she was still in bed. I would then sit on the edge of her bed and we would have lovely chats together.

I often found her reading the Bible when I entered her room. She would ask about school and how I was doing; she brought a real sense of calm to our house. While she stayed with us, my father was always on his best behaviour. He would stay home at night and act like the perfect gentleman. If only he had been like that all the time.

With no alcohol he was like a different person. I was always sad to see her leave after her holiday was over, as I knew the day she left, my father would be drinking again.

I often wished she would stay for good.

Christmas cheer...
The only other time my father was on his best behaviour, was when we were in the town. If we were meeting other people with children, he would pretend he was a great father and would always go and buy sweets for them. He was brilliant at putting on a good public show.

Even at Christmas time we were never allowed a tree but every year I used to open a box of Christmas decorations that I found in the spare bedroom. The box was full of tinsel, baubles and

Christmas ornaments. It was all old stuff, probably gathered up over the years by a previous generation but the sparkle and shine would lift my spirits.

Inside the box was a set of lights that I just loved. When I would switch them on I would sit and admire their beauty. It was amazing, each light was different. From a choir boy, to a carriage, to a Santa's head, to a Christmas house. I never saw lights like them, and never have since. I knew they should be on a tree but since that was out of the question, this was the next best thing. Over Christmas I would go and plug in the lights and just sit and enjoy them.

I remember with sadness one Christmas Eve when a family came to visit, a mother and her two daughters. My father had been drinking that day and was very merry. One of the girls saw the lights and started to admire them, so my father told her she could have them. I was absolutely devastated. He knew I loved them, they were the only thing I enjoyed about Christmas. He watched me every year, taking them out of their box, enjoying their beauty yet still, he gave them away.

Christmas came and went every year. It was a time of year that should be a happy occasion for children but I grew to hate it. It just was an excuse for my father to drink more. People would bring him whiskey for presents, so along with his usual amount to drink, he had extra.

Every Christmas was the same story; he would be drunk every day. Then he would go to the local town and meet his drinking buddies. As it was Christmas, they bought each other a drink, so arguments and sleepless nights were the norm over Christmas. I was so glad when it was all over and things would return to some kind of normality. I wanted fewer scenes of my father lying lifeless on the floor, and less tension in the house.

Chapter Three

BOMBING THE WHISKEY FACTORIES

My father continued to drink heavily and arguments in the house with him and my uncles were frequent. He would attend every social gathering he could, especially funerals and would always return very drunk. The fights were always about alcohol and where the money was coming from to buy it each week. He went out drinking most nights as well. The smell of stale cigarettes and whiskey lingering in the air made my stomach churn.

I was glad our house was big, as there were lots of places I could hide. Never did anyone question where I was. I often prayed to God to put a bomb under the whiskey factories, when the factories were empty of people, so nobody would get hurt. All the whiskey could drain down into the sewers and I would have my father back.

Not much for a little girl to ask, and if carefully planned, nobody would get hurt, and my world would be a much happier place. My prayer, if answered would have solved all of my family's problems.

Every week I watched my uncle giving money to my father to do the shopping and pay the household bills. I could not understand why he kept giving it to him but my father would use his wit and charm to make sure he got it. The pattern was always the same. My father had money, he would go to town and bring back a little food and be drunk. My uncle would then confront him over the bills not being paid. It was a never-ending cycle. I could not understand why my uncle would not take charge of the affairs himself and put an end to the problem.

My father smoked heavily too and always had an answer for my uncle about the cost of living and how everything was so expensive, that was why he wasn't paying the bills. But it was clear to see, even though money was very scarce, he always had money for his whiskey and cigarettes.

I remember many times telling my father my feet were hurting badly, as my shoes were too tight. My shoes would have to be completely worn out before being replaced, not bought because my feet were growing. I had a lot of pain and would often search out old, worn shoes and cut the toes out of them just so I could wear them around the house. I remember in school, a foot specialist coming on one occasion and fitting me with insoles to try and relieve my pain. But because my shoes were so tight, it was easier not to wear them.

Sundays at the pub...
Often my father would bring me and my brother to the pub; usually after church on a Sunday. He would insist we go with him and I hated it. It was never very busy at that time, but the men who we met were often drunk. Stinking of whiskey and staggering about, their words were slurred and often didn't make any sense.

They were my father's friends so it didn't surprise me that he got on so well with them as they were living the same life. I wonder now, what their families lives were like, were they the same as ours? It made no sense to me, that my father would make sure to take us to church on a Sunday, say our prayers and then take us off to the pub afterwards. He would not let us take part in any of the church activities like Girl Guides or for my brother, Boy Scouts. I know now, it was all control.

If people really knew what our lives were like behind closed doors, would we have been left in the family? He made sure he had full control over our lives so no stories could be carried, and nobody could find out the real truth. To the outside world it must have looked like I had the perfect life, living in a large Georgian house, set on a big farm. As I was the only girl, people probably thought I was spoilt but the truth was, my life was a living hell. I was young and trapped in a very hard place but I knew it would not always be that way. I would grow up and get away and make my own life choices, good choices that would not destroy my loved ones.

Dead in a ditch...

After Granny Alice died, my father's drinking became a bigger problem. He went to town every night for his fill. The neighbours were very good and gave him lifts to the pub as it was close to a main road. I was always I was always afraid that he would stagger out in front of a car and cause an accident which may have destroyed another family.

As a child, I would often sit waiting at the bedroom window if my father had not returned home. On the bedroom wall hung a diamond-shaped picture of a vase filled with flowers. With the light of the moon, the mother of pearl vase would glisten. I sat and studied that picture most nights and often wished I could paint like that.

I would start to get anxious about his whereabouts. I was always scared he could be dead in a ditch and not coming home. I waited every night for him and would be relieved to eventually see him staggering slowly up the avenue, with the moon giving light to his path. I would thank God for bringing him safely home and I would creep back to my bed and try to get some sleep.

If my father was going around the house banging doors and shouting, sleep was very scarce. It was a spooky house and yet i'm sure a lovely house in its day, but now it was very different. The remains of a tennis court was at the front of the house. I often wondered about the family who lived in the house before us. They must have been rich, to own a house like this. But now the walls were musty and damp.

The floors were timber and a room at the end of the corridor was out of bounds because the floor was rotten and gaping holes were appearing. Buckets and cloths were placed in the hall to catch the water that came through the roof on a wet day. The buckets filled very quickly when it rained. It saddened me to see that nothing was being done to repair any of the problems, but then again, with my father buying whiskey every day, how could there be money to spend on anything else?

A pile of roof slates lay on one side of the front door, purchased by my grandfather to mend the roof - I'm sure that pile is still in the same place today. I did paint my bedroom and the bathroom at one point and made pretty curtains by hand for the bathroom window. The floor in the bathroom was rotten too but at least the room looked pretty.

We had a bath and a very fancy, round patterned sink. The pattern was blue and very busy. The sink was held in a wooden surround which was rotting. The sink had tilted in the frame because there was lack of support. I thought one day there will be a loud crash, as the sink would come falling through the floor down to the room below.

I wondered at times if the house was haunted as it was always so cold and chilly, and some of the walls had sections of green slime running down them from the damp. There were many times as a young girl that I would feel awful fear in that house. It was certainly not a suitable home for us. The washing facilities were very basic. The bathroom had a steel bath and only cold water came from both taps. Washing in a basin was the only option. Hot water was got from kettles hanging over the fireplace in the kitchen. Clothes were washed in a top-loader washing machine and either hung outside to dry or in the kitchen by the heat of the fire. In the cold days of winter, sitting by the fire, droplets of water would fall on my head from the wet clothes hanging above. A damp musty smell would fill the room after a few days, as the clothes would take so long to dry.

Chapter Four

My Plan

One morning I woke to the sound of birdsong outside my window, it was early spring. Despite the heartbreak I was living in, I took comfort in the nature around me. I lay in bed, covered by a wool blanket and I watched my breath rise in the air like smoke. The bedroom was so cold, the breath from my body was warmer than the air around me.

The night before, my father had come home from town very drunk and had been up most of the night banging doors and staggering about the house. It was nights like these, that I lay curled up under the blankets praying to God he would not come into my room. I had witnessed his anger and rage so many times in his drunken state, I had learned to avoid him. It was harder to get away from him when he came into my room. I had got little sleep and knew my uncles hadn't got much either, so I decided to come up with a plan.

My plan was I could help uncle James do the grocery shopping. This would solve our problem as he would no longer be giving my father money. Bills would now be paid and my father would have less money to buy whiskey and cigarettes. He would have to cut back and that could only be a good thing.

I went downstairs and looked inside the kitchen cupboards, I was going to make up my shopping list. The cupboards in the kitchen were old and full of woodworm and always had a bad smell. The doors were worn and chipped and the hinges were loose and rusty from the damp. As I searched in the cupboards, I realised what little of food I found proved we didn't eat a lot. I made up my list as best as I could and decided I needed to choose carefully the right time to approach my uncle.

My idea was very simple. I would push the trolley and my uncle would fill it with what we needed. I did worry a little if I would be tall enough and strong enough to push the trolley, but I knew we would manage. All I had to do now, was explain to uncle James how my plan would work. I plucked up the courage to speak with him for I knew he was not in very good form. He was very quiet in himself and was busy in the kitchen getting something to eat. I watched him walking into the dining room to eat his breakfast.

The dining room was off the kitchen; it was a large room filled with a table. Long wooden benches were the seating at both sides and a large dresser filled one corner. The doors on the dresser had little glass panels, most of which were cracked or just the frames existed - it had seen better days. The room was cold and the walls were green with damp. A small four-bar heater was the only heat source and that was only plugged in if the frost was on the ground outside. Money was tight so an electric heater was a luxury item.

I needed to pick up the courage to speak to Uncle James, he was the older one who had the chequebook. He had often made it clear to me, that my brother's views were important but I was to be seen and not heard. I was only a little girl living in these men's world.

As soon as I heard my uncle pouring his tea, I went in and sat across from him at the table. His head was bowed and he seemed to be totally concentrating on getting his tea over so he could get on with his day. He looked so weary, but then we all were. Not getting sleep, constant arguments in the house and constant worry about what would become of the family was taking its toll. Of course my father was the main problem, but we were powerless to do anything about it. Money was scarce and when the farm animals were sold they were not being replaced. It was only a matter of time before the farm would have to be sold. The future was not looking good!

I took a deep breath and told him about my plan. He looked into his teacup the whole time I spoke. I blurted the words out as quickly as I could and waited for his answer. He startled me as his reply came quickly. I could tell by his expression he was not impressed by an eight-year-old girl giving him advice on his affairs. He looked at me and in an angry voice cursed me up and down saying: "Mind your own business!"

I left the room quickly as my uncle scared me when he spoke to me like that. I was so disappointed that my plan had failed. I couldn't understand why my uncle was so mean to me. He seemed so helpless to take control and stop my father having such easy access to money that he clearly could not handle. Even though my uncle was older than my father my father had such power over him which he used through manipulation. yet my father had such power over him. I doubted things would ever change. I had to think of a plan B now, something had to be done before my family was destroyed from the rot caused by alcohol.

The same story just a different day...
That day the atmosphere in the house was really bad, it was late afternoon before I heard my father coming down the stairs and he was angry. Few words were spoken as he busied himself getting something to eat. I could hear him mumbling away to himself. His brothers stayed out of his way, which was the usual after a bad night. When he ate his food he left the plates at the washing-up basin. I sat in silence in the kitchen, pretending to read a newspaper. It was easier to busy myself to avoid making conversation with him. Usually if I spoke to him under the influence of alcohol, his words would be very nasty so silence was a better option.

He left the kitchen and I could hear him taking his coat and scarf from the large mahogany coat stand in the hallway. The stand always creaked with the weight of coats that hung on it. He was getting himself ready to go back to town again for more alcohol. Soon he appeared back in the kitchen and told me he was going to town. I hid behind the paper I was reading and never answered.

Before I had often asked him to stay at home, but I was always sharply told that he would do what he liked.

He closed the kitchen door behind him as he left and I put down the paper. It saddened me that the pub had a bigger attraction to him than spending some quality time with his children. It seemed like all he ever did was walk out and leave. Thoughts went through my head of the night that lay ahead. He would return drunk again; little sleep would be had. Arguments would continue, it would be the same story just a different day.

I heard the chatter in the scullery of my uncles' voices as they came in from working outside on the farm. I needed to make myself scarce. They would be cross that my father was gone into town again. I didn't need to be listening to this. They were the ones who were giving my father the money to drink. They were part of the problem and were prepared to do nothing about it.

I left the kitchen, gently placing the latch on the door behind me. I would go upstairs and sit quietly in the bedroom and read a book. My days were long and very lonely. As darkness descended I sat by the window. The air outside was frosty. The glass on the window was very thin and as night descended the frost particles would attach to the glass and by morning the most beautiful patterns would emerge. I wrapped myself in a blanket and in the darkness watched the stars. Soon the moon appeared in all its glory, as the cars travelled past on the road. I wondered when my father would return home. I prayed to God he would come home safely.

That night, I sat waiting for him in the chair by the window in his bedroom. The moon was shining bright, lighting the front field outside. It cast light where I sat beside the wardrobe. I often wondered what was kept in the wardrobe as my father always kept it firmly locked. I saw a car stop at the gate and a figure getting out. The car drove away; some kind person had brought him home again. In the moonlight, I watched him staggering up the steep lane waving his arms about. It was clear he was drunk, so I went into bed.

I got little sleep as he banged on the door and shouted angry words until tiredness overcame him. I hated what drink was doing to my home, my father was the only father I had and I wanted the best for him. This was the pattern on many nights. He was totally consumed and controlled by his addiction to alcohol.

I always worried about what would happen if my father died while I was young. So many times I had found him drunk and worried that he might stop breathing. I would watch his lifeless body as a little girl and pray his chest would rise so I knew he was alive, afraid to waken him in case I got an angry outburst. Bad and all as he was, he was my father. So many days he could not be a father because his life was consumed by his addiction. He was absent from his responsibilities as a single parent. I was worried because my uncles always favoured my brother - what would happen to me? My uncle David often got angry and would always swear at me and call me names. I would often dream of my father's funeral and wake up in a cold sweat. These dreams were probably fuelled by my fears for his life. My uncles were caught up in my father's addiction, they were too powerless to stand up and look after themselves. They were victims too. An addiction affects the whole family and it was very clear our family was being torn apart.

Chapter Five

MY MOTHER

My heart went out to him many times, as I felt he was living his hell here on earth. Often when he was drunk he would cry buckets of tears, I often wondered why he did that to himself. Was he lonely due to his failed marriage?

I have not mentioned my mother yet. This is because she was not with us at home. As a child I didn't understand I even had a mother that cared for me. As I got older I questioned my father about her and all he would tell me was that she was useless. He would say that she walked out and left him with two children to raise on his own. He often said that she did not care for me or my brother. His favourite words to use, which he told me many times, was that: 'When my brother was born she wasn't happy and then when I was born she still wasn't happy, so she left.'

I often wondered if it was all my fault she was not in our lives. Did she leave after I was born because I was not the child she wanted? What my father told me made sense at the time as she never came to visit our home. Her name was never spoken by anyone in the family. She did send us birthday and Christmas presents but that was it.

I remember very occasional visits to Dublin to see her. We would travel by train to meet her at Houston station and visit the zoo. It was a real novelty to get a day out, the excitement of going on a train, and of course my father would be as sober as a judge. He had to be on his best behaviour. I remember one day at the zoo walking at a distance behind my mother and father, my brother and I busy eating ice cream and enjoying the animals. I could not hear what my parents were saying to each other but I did see my father raising his hand up and pointing his finger at my mother, as if he was making his point to her loud and clear. I was too busy enjoying my day to notice anything else.

My mother was a stranger in my life. She was living in Dublin and never made much of an effort to be a part of our lives, so my father's words of how she didn't care for us made perfect sense to me. He wasn't an easy man to live with but he was all we had. I accepted this was my lot in life and I would get on with it. Life would not always be this way. I would grow up and have my own life, but for now I was helpless to do anything or change the people around me.

School life...

We went to a local National School which was less than half a mile away so we could walk there. It was a Catholic school and we were Church of Ireland. Often on school mornings we would quietly sneak out of the house, with no breakfast or lunch after being awake most of the night, because of our drunken father.

The headmaster in the school would often take pity and share his lunch with me. Other children in the school would laugh and jeer me because I had no mother. They were very cruel with their words about her. I had enough one day and thought I would find a photograph of her and prove them wrong. I did have a mother; I would show them. She walked out and left me but they didn't need to know that, I just needed to prove that she existed.

When I got home that day, I searched through the metal chest in the sitting room where the photographs were kept - I would show them! I very carefully found a nice photo of her on their wedding day. My hands were shaking, for if my father knew I was showing her photograph he would not be pleased. As far as he was concerned she had no value in our lives.

The next day, after taking it with me to school, I made sure to put the photograph back exactly where I found it. I was terrified my father would find out, as her name was taboo in our home. If I ever spoke of her I would be in trouble.

Odd one out...

As the school was Catholic we were the odd ones out. I am not sure if it was the school or my father who decided to exclude us from the Religious Education classes, but we were not allowed to participate.

I remember so well the days of those classes. Just before they began, the room would fall silent and the teacher would then wait for me to leave. I would gather my books and my bag and as I closed the door behind me, the voices would start again. I hated it, I was being rejected from the class and couldn't understand why.

I had done nothing, but I was being treated differently for the whole class to see. I never made any friends in National School, but the fact I was made out to be so different from the other kids probably didn't help. When I had a bad day in school and went home to tell my father he would tell me not to be carrying stories and would refuse to listen. It was those days that I spent all my time with our farm dog. He was a very gentle and sweet natured blue/grey sheepdog named Rover. Many days we would walk the fields and I would chat away to him. He was a great listener and loved to hear all my stories about school. We were the best of friends.

My father made sure I had no other friends so I was glad I had Rover. Our next-door neighbours were Church of Ireland and had a girl the same age as me. Her mother was always asking me to go along to things in the church but my father would not allow it. I now know this was more control on his part. If I did not mix with people, his life was private. I would not be at risk of speaking out about what our lives were really like at home.

Changing my name...

I will never forget one day that I returned home from school and my father was in the kitchen waiting for me. I could see instantly by his face he was in a bad mood, his breath had a strong smell of whiskey and he was drunk. I was scared, I knew something bad was going to happen.

I gasped loudly as he leapt towards me and grabbed the school bag on my back. He pulled me really hard taking my bag from me and insisting I emptied the contents out. I couldn't understand what he was looking for, I had nothing to hide. He took one of my books that had my name written on the front of it, he then searched for a biro from my pencil case and started to scribble my name out. He was very angry and scored over my name with great gusto. I was terrified about what he was going to do next.

My Christian name, Ann, was taken from the first part of my mothers name, Annette. He told me I was never to spell my name in that way again. He warned me from that day on, I was to spell it properly or else change it completely! I didn't argue or ask why. He was so angry I was afraid to question him. What was the big deal? My name was fine as far as I was concerned. Yes it might be more common to add an 'e' to the end but I was used to it just the way it was. With the information I found out in later years, I wonder was he trying to erase my mother from my life in every way he could? It was obvious he hated her.

Chapter Six

Cruel Times

I learned to be seen and not heard a lot of the time. It was more peaceful and easier for me to exist with my animals than it was to put up with the fighting and unrest in my family. The animals at home didn't get much care either. Our poor donkey always had curled-up feet. I thought all donkeys feet were like that, until I got older and realised it was due to neglect by not keeping his hooves trimmed. He must have been in terrible pain.

Any new dog they got would be collared and a chain would be wrapped around a tyre, and the dog would drag the tyre around with him. I thought as a child there must be another way to train a dog but any suggestions I made to release the dog from the tyre were met with the usual response of: "Mind your own business!"

My brother was also cruel on his visits back to the farm from college. I was sickened by his attitude of laying poison to kill everything from a dog to a bird, to protect the young lambs. I often thought that he could just keep an eye on them and then he wouldn't have to put down poison. It sickened me to see how easy this was for him, he seemed to be getting a kick out of it. I remember him telling me that some of the sheep were badly attacked by dogs, they were in shock and in pain. He went on to say he was withdrawing the medication from them so it would be okay in a few days to have them slaughtered for the freezer. I left the room feeling sick. How could he do this to an animal, let it suffer in this way? I could not believe we both grew up in the same house but could think so differently. Where was his heart, his compassion? We were so different but I was thankful for that; I spoke to him about my views but he was not keen to listen.

I didn't have a close relationship with Michael so I was very lonely at home. I developed a great love for the animals, especially our sheepdog Rover. Many a tear was shed into his coat and he would look into my eyes as if to say he understood my pain. My uncle David in a bad humour would often lash out and kick him, just because he could. Other times, he chased kittens around the yard with a pitchfork, trying to stab them as I pleaded with him to stop. He thought this was good fun. I screamed at him with tears streaming down my face, shocked by his needless and heartless cruelty. He did eventually stop and thankfully the kittens scattered into their hiding places unhurt. He walked away laughing at the upset he had caused. What kind of a person would get fun out of animal cruelty?

I wondered how kind my uncles were to the animals when I was at school. At one point I was told they tied a dog to a gate, hanging it by its back legs and then they pulled its teeth out. Thank God I wasn't around to witness this. They thought this was funny. It broke my heart that they were so cruel and as a child I was too helpless and scared to do anything about it.

All of uncle David's behaviour was malicious, he verbally attacked me on a daily basis. I never remember one kind word from his lips to me. On many occasions he would swear at me and call me names. He made it very clear that I wasn't wanted in his home. I was just a child and was of no use to him.

He was also physically abusive towards me. I remember one day when the cattle broke out, he caught my arm and pushed me against a live electric fence. He held me against it to check its strength. The pain was unbearable as the shocks went through my body, it was a sensation I will never forget. He laughed at me in my distress as he thought it was very funny. I was distraught and cried loudly, yet he did not care his actions had caused this pain.

When I was upset like this I had nobody to comfort me. It was in these moments that the reality of my living situation became very real. I was being abused by my uncle David, uncle James ignored me, my brother wasn't interested and my father was drunk. All my father did was leave me, he was more interested in alcohol than what was happening to his daughter. I felt so alone.

I put on a lot of weight at one point. I developed an awful fear of being left with nothing to eat, so I found comfort in food. White bread and jam was my primary food. I always loved to bake but anything I ever made was ridiculed. My uncle James would very quickly tell me that my baking *tasted like poison* and he couldn't eat it. Yet he always did. I often wondered if it was that bad, then why was he eating it? A compliment would have been nice and yes, my cooking probably wasn't the best, but I was a child who was keen to learn.

The weight of humiliation...
On one of our rare Sunday visits to the local shop, we met a neighbour. He invited us back to his house for tea. He was a farmer and lived with his mother and sister. We sat in the kitchen and my father chatted away. As time went on it was suggested I should be taken out to the cow shed to be weighed, as I was so heavy. I was horrified but believed that they were only joking. However they were very serious. His mother insisted I was to go on the scales, she said I was too fat. I felt so embarrassed. I didn't want to be paraded out to the shed to see what weight I was. I couldn't believe it when my father agreed with her and ordered me outside.

It was a cold night, I was only dressed in shorts and a t-shirt so I shivered as we crossed the yard. I didn't know if it was the cold air or the fear of humiliation but my teeth started to chatter. My father lifted me and stood me on the scales that were used to weigh the bags of grain. As the weights were added on one side, the comments were made on how heavy I was. They kept adding the weights to the tray until the needle came to the proper place on the dial.

I was mortified. They all huddled around me and thought this was so funny; the general consensus was; I was too fat. I felt so humiliated and degraded. My brother took great delight in my embarrassment and didn't let me forget it for a long time afterwards.

Chapter Seven

Farm Life

I was very thankful to have the farm animals as companions. On the lonely days I would spend time with my loved Rover. We played and chatted the long days away. I loved all the animals and spent a lot of time caring for them. We had a handful of cows; the milk they produced was strained and put into a silver milk churn and taken down to the road on a rusty trolley for the milkman to collect. The job of milking the cows was often given to me.

The milking shed was across the yard from the house. It was an open shed with byres where the cows would be tied loosely with a chain to be milked. They would stand quietly and let me put the chain around their neck, chewing their cud knowing that in a little while, I would lighten their load of milk.

Every cow would enter the same byre for milking time. It was amusing to watch them coming into the shed and taking up their rightful place. Often it meant they would move around each other in such a gentle way, to make sure each one ended up in their rightful place. Bringing in the cows for milking was a major job. They were kept in a field which was not beside the house, it was a little further down the road. The cattle had access to the woods, making it even harder to find them as they could be anywhere. My faithful dog, Rover, helped me gather them together and sometimes the yard cats, all five of them would come along too. I was like the Pied Piper with a trail of animals coming behind me.

At milking time the cats would line up at the back of the cows and wait for their treat. I would spray milk at them straight from the cow. It was amusing watching them licking the milk from their chests. Some milk would go into their mouth but most of it ran down their coats to be enjoyed later. They would lick their paws and rub their faces with a look of pure contentment on their faces.

Milking was done by hand. The cows were all very placid. They would stand with their eyes half-closed, chewing their cud. Sometimes a cow, while being milked would shuffle about and end up with a hoof in the bucket. After a little gentle coaxing, the hoof would be removed along with the bucket and milking would start afresh.

In the spring, baby lambs would arrive. Often if a lamb was very weak it would be brought into the kitchen and placed in a box, in front of the Aga cooker. I loved nursing them back to health. I would see their tiny bodies, with fear in their eyes and have to coax them to drink warm milk from a bottle. When they were staying in the kitchen I used to sneak down in the middle of the night, when all was quiet to look after them. Every step I took on the wooden stairs creaked under my feet. I would warm some milk and give it to the little creature curled up in the cardboard box. It was such a pleasure to see a little lamb that looked lifeless the night before, spring into action and be reunited with its mother the next day. My uncle would always tell me off for getting up in the middle of the night and making enough noise to wake up the whole house. This was a joke to me, as when my father was drunk and shouting his head off till four or five in the morning. I was caring for his animals and he still had to complain at me.

Winter in the house was so cold with no heating. We only had an Aga and an open fire in the kitchen. The bedrooms were always cold and damp; I would heat my body in the kitchen and then run to my bedroom, tucking up in bed as fast as possible.

Often in my youth I had to find ways to pass the time at home. After my homework was finished and I didn't need to milk the

Farm Life

cows, I was free. I would play games of snakes and ladders or ludo with my imaginary friend. Snap, with a pack of cards was a good option too and of course, I always won. Well I suppose, what did it matter if I cheated a bit. There was no television to watch and when tensions were high in the house I would go to my bedroom and read an old comic that was lying around. Sometimes my father would bring home a comic for me and a boys magazine for my brother. In the pictures I would see families on day trips to the sea, picnics with friends, holiday images of candy floss and donkey rides. My world was miles apart from the happy family images on the pages. I didn't see images of drunken parents, children living in fear with no security or love. It was like a different world than the one I lived in.

I often thought about sneaking Rover into the house for company, but I knew if I did and he was found inside we would be punished. He was an outside dog and that's where he would stay. I felt I had no value in my family but I knew in my Creator's eyes I was special and had a purpose. I would lose my thoughts doing little projects of embroidery that my kind neighbour had given me. I would create pretty flowers and patterns on fabric no bigger than a handkerchief.

I loved to see the lambs playing in the field. Some years there would be a pet lamb that would have to be fed with a bottle, as its mother had not enough milk or had died. I loved these little guys, they always remained pets as they grew. If I went out to the field, they would come running up for a greeting and a bit of fuss. It was amusing to go to the field full of sheep and call out. The pets would raise their heads and come running.

I remember as a little girl coming home from school one day and the sheep were held in a pen in the yard getting ready to be sheared. I went in and did my homework. Later that evening I went to the back door to feed Rover. I opened the door and went out to put food in the bowl. All I heard was sheep baaing and I could hear the noise of the shearing machine in the distance. I had been warned to stay away while the men were shearing. I fed the dog and turned to go back to the house. I froze; an animal was approaching with great gusto. It had black legs, a black face and a sheared body. I was frozen to the spot. What on earth was it? I was terrified and screamed at the top of my voice.

My father appeared at the door and laughed. He told me it was the pet lamb I had the year before. I felt like a right fool, but it looked so different. Its lovely fleece had gone and now it looked ridiculous with its long spindly legs, a pot belly and no fleece but it was still delighted to see me.

Returning home...
When I was in secondary school my friends were very good to me. Some weekends I would go out with them to their homes and they treated me as one of their own family. I was very grateful to them as during this time I was suffering awful pain with my feet. I had problems with ingrown toenails and had badly blistered feet. My father's opinion was if the shoes looked okay then I didn't need new ones, even though my feet were still growing. Comfort was not an issue. Little did I know then, that this neglect would cause serious problems later in my life. I learned to be thankful for every day knowing that my life would not always be this way and to expect nothing. This way I could cope with my life.

Other weekends I stayed at school. I would sit at the dorm window watching parents hugging their children, I saw their delight when they saw their offspring. I was never jealous or envious of them, just sad that my family was so different. At the end of term, I would get a lift home from one of the parents who lived nearby. Most times I returned to an empty house; my uncles were out on the farm and my father at the pub. I would just switch off from the pain. Another day arriving home from school and no one to welcome me. I longed for the day when my life would change.

The men always smoked cigarettes in the house so I could never get the stench of cigarettes off my clothes. It seemed to be engrained in the fibres of the fabric, probably a result of being hung dripping wet in the kitchen for days. I was thankful to the people who would drive my father home at night so that he was safe but often they would come in and drink with him until the early hours of the morning. I could hear the sound of their drunken laughter and chatter and would try to get to sleep but knew next morning the sitting room would be stinking of stale cigarettes and whiskey, and the table would be littered with empty bottles and cigarette butts. I was thankful that my father never drove.

I often thought of the families of the men who drank with my father. Were their children and wives living in abuse also due to drink?

The Vintage Festival...
In the summer holidays one year I met my school friends in a local hotel. The town was holding a Vintage Festival. I knew my father was in the town too but to my horror he turned up at the hotel. It was always a week my father would be drunk every day. The pubs were always busy during this time, so my father was in his element. On the last day I was to meet a few of my friends who lived in the local area. They were my secondary school friends who would be heading back to college a month later for a new term together. We were sitting together in the foyer of the hotel. I looked up and at the door stood my father, he knew I was going to be there. I could see he was very drunk, he was waving his arms about and propped himself up in the doorway. I was mortified. What was he doing? How dare he come in a state like this and embarrass me in front of my friends. I worried they wouldn't remain my friends if they knew I had a drunk for a father.

I sat watching what he would do. He staggered over towards us barely able to put one foot in front of the other, then he fell in a heap on the ground. That was it, I could take no more. I had kept my father's drinking abuse a secret from them, but now what would they think? I got up and left the hotel feeling so alone and stuck in a bad place. I was crying, feeling so sad and disappointed with my father for his total lack of respect for me.

I really wanted to have a dad that I could be proud of. This is not the way my life was supposed to be. My friends had 'normal' fathers who weren't drunks - they were hardworking, respectable men providing for their family.

Chapter Eight

My Faithful Rover

After I left National School I was sent away to boarding school, which was forty miles away. My brother had already gone there a few years before me and we both hated it. I felt I was being sent away because I was in the way of my father's social life. I didn't get home, except at end of term and the only reason I wanted to come home was to see Rover.

He would always be sitting on the front lawn when I came home. He would come running, delighted to see me. On the journey home I always looked forward to the welcome he would give me. I could always depend on him to be happy to see me on my return.

This time as the car turned in the drive I could not see Rover. I thanked the lady who had driven me home and got my bag from the boot. Deep inside I knew that something was wrong. I went around the back of the house and looked in the shed where Rover had his bed but it was empty. I dropped my bag and ran into the house.

My father was washing dishes in the kitchen and my uncles sat each side of the fireplace watching a small fire smouldering in the grate. I asked them where Rover was. My uncles never uttered a word as I waited for a reply. Then my father spoke and said very coldly 'he is dead'. I turned and went out to the yard to get my bag. Tears welled in my eyes. My four-legged friend was gone, I was broken-hearted.

To my father and uncles he was only an old outside dog. To me, he was my best friend. They laughed at me in my grief. My uncle went on to tell me Rover had died down by the river. That was where he found his body, it was a place I used to go to play with him. I would throw sticks into the shallow water and he would jump in and bring them back to me. It was our fun place away from all the arguments, abuse and pain. I wondered, if that was why he went back to that place to die. My heart was broken.

The next morning, I felt I had to visit the place where Rover was found. I left the house leaving an argument behind me. My father had been so drunk the night before, little sleep was got by anyone so the atmosphere was not good. I would get out and have some peace and deal with my grief in my own way. They didn't care or understand the love I had for him.

The sun was warm on my back as I climbed the gate into the wood. Tears streamed down my face as I remembered all the times I walked the same path with my four-legged friend. Today I walked alone, picking any wild flowers I could find in the grass. As I entered the wood a soft breeze was blowing. The sunlight was dancing to light my path as the trees swayed above. Sadness hit me as I knew I had lost the best friend I'd ever had in that place. We shared our lives and now he was gone.

The day was closing in so I knew I had better get home before too long. I got to the edge of the wood and stood. It was so peaceful as the birds sang in the trees above me.

The evening sun was shining and casting shadows at my feet and in the distance I could hear the water flowing in the river. I walked through the long grass, avoiding the thistles and nettles that seemed to bend towards me as I approached picking lovely flowers.

As I came to the river I could hear the soft flow of the water, it was summer so the level of the river was low. I stood at the place I knew so well. A flat stone lay nearby. This stone was often a good place for me to sit as Rover played around me. Often he would come out of the water and wait until he was beside me before he shook the water from his coat. Often I ended up being nearly as wet as he was but that didn't matter for love shows affection.

I carefully laid the flowers that I had gathered on the water and watched them drift away. Sometimes I noticed they would get stuck on a stone but not for long as the water would soon carry them away. My tears ran easily as each flower disappearing was like a memory of Rover and me. I was now alone.

I did think if my family knew what I was doing they would laugh and call me stupid but to them that was my middle name. Rover showed only love and care for me and this was my tribute to him. I left the river, with the sound of running water disappearing into the distance and went back through the wood and composed myself. I did not want to return to the house upset, I did not want to give them any reason to laugh or jeer me in my loss. They were heartless men never showing love or compassion to a human so why was I surprised they had no understanding of me in my grief?

I lifted the latch on the back door and I could hear voices in the kitchen, my uncles were still sitting, one each side of the fire chatting. They told me my father had gone to town for the night. I said goodnight, went to bed and I cried myself to sleep.

Protection and hope...
The next day, my uncles were out working on the farm and my father had gone to town for his usual session. I had some bread and jam and went to my bedroom. Sitting on the bed I prayed life would get better. Life would go on, I would be able to cope and somehow it would get better.

As the evening came I could hear my uncles chattering in the kitchen below. I got into bed and lay in the darkness thinking of the lonely day I just had. The hours passed and I heard a car stop at the gate. This was probably some kind neighbour dropping my drunken father home - guess what, I was right.

My father in his drunken state was often abusive to me. My brother pulled him off me one night when he attacked in a drunken stupor asking me to give him a watch my mother had sent me as a birthday present. I refused to give it to him and he started beating me about my head and face.

On another occasion he threw a hairdryer at me. It hit me on the head and split me open. I learned when he was drunk and angry my best defence was to stay out of his way. He lived always denying he had a problem with drink. I suppose it was the only way he could survive in this world.

I sang *'Jesus loves me this I know'* through tears of sadness. I know God didn't blow up the whiskey factories, he didn't stop my father drinking, but he did give a little girl protection and hope. I always knew my life didn't have to go the same way. I could make a choice, I had free will to do so. I made a promise to myself one day, after I saw my father's body lying on the sitting room floor, so much alcohol in it that he had been sick, wet himself and had no movement in his entire body. I thought he was dead. I made a promise to myself that day that I would never put any of my loved ones through the pain he was putting his family through. What a choice to make as a child.

Many times my uncles would enter the bedroom carrying my father's lifeless body and just leave him on the floor. I would hide under the covers, pretending to be asleep. When they were gone, I would get up and cover his body with a blanket and pray to God he would be alive in the morning. I would lay awake listening to his breathing and only when I could no longer stay awake, drift into a sleep.

Usually when I returned from school on those days my uncles would be outside and my father would be up busying himself in the kitchen as if all was normal. His cooking skills were okay when he was sober but if he was preparing food while drinking then often the old dinners would be mixed in with new dinners in a saucepan. I would be so hungry I would eat it without complaint. It was easier to be quiet and accept the way things were than complain and risk a violent outburst.

Chapter Nine

WATERING IT DOWN

Due to the alcoholism I had witnessed I vowed I never would drink. To help my father I became an expert at watering down whiskey with red lemonade. House plants often got watered with whiskey until it killed them or the stench got so bad I had to change plan. My father never knew, he always came home so drunk from town he wouldn't know what he was drinking.

My father one day in a drunken state complained I didn't know how to enjoy myself because I didn't drink. He laughed at me and said I would have to marry a man who only drank water. My reply to him was that I would marry a man who had a healthy respect for alcohol and then I quickly left the room.

I thank God every day for the wisdom he gave me to stand strong as a young girl; he gave me strong morals and also protection. So many times my father was in a drunken rage and I managed to get away from him without harm.

I decided after my Inter Cert exam I would leave school. My brother had left and had gone to work in England. I was never really close to my brother. His ways were often very odd but maybe that was his way of coping. If there was trouble at home, he would often just walk out and leave me to fend for myself. I was deeply unhappy in school and just wanted out.

My ideal profession was nursing. Some of my friends were

going to do nursing but had the love and support of their family to do it. I knew I would never have that in my life. My secondary school was totally funded by grants. My father never took a job - he was just bleeding my uncles dry and they were powerless to stop him.

I felt if I could get a job I could take care of myself, so I applied for and got a job in Sandymount area in Dublin. It gave me accommodation and money in my pocket to pay my way. It would also give me a chance to get to know my mother better.

I moved to Dublin but found it very hard to settle in the city. My mother was living in a small bed-sit flat and had a job caring for an old lady. She asked us to have tea with her one afternoon so I got the bus into town and met my mother.

We walked a short distance to her home, she lived over the family business which was a pub. We met her son behind the bar and my mother introduced me to him. He spoke a few words and said his mother was expecting us. We left the bar and climbed the narrow stairs. Which had crates of minerals lined up one side.

My mother knocked on the door and a voice told us to enter. A little old lady sat on a huge chair in the corner of the room. She welcomed us kindly and served us a lovely tea. My mother spoke very kindly to her and they had a laugh together.

I enjoyed that time with my mother. We didn't speak of family things and the only thing she told me was, she could not stay with my father because of his drinking. At my age I did not understand fully what she meant, but I did wonder how she could walk away and leave two vulnerable children in his care.

I felt however it was better not to say anything so I kept my thoughts to myself. My father's words rang in my ears of how my mother 'was useless' and 'didn't care for us' and that was why she left us. I felt sorry for my mother living in a little bed-sit and I knew her health was not good. She was visiting doctors and the hospital a lot so I felt it was best to keep the peace between us.

I left Dublin four months later and returned home as city life was not for me. I was lonely in unfamiliar territory, and felt I could not resolve the issues of my past with my mother. My mother was sad to hear of my decision. The day I left on the train she came with me to the station.

Few words were spoken between us, I said goodbye to her on the platform and gave her a hug. She was upset to see me leave and even now, I can still picture her standing outside the carriage I was in, waving me off with tears streaming down her face. It was now me leaving her.

I returned home to arguments and my father was still drinking heavily. Nothing had changed, the same rot and dysfunction was still there.

My uncles were victims of circumstance as I was, and were powerless to take a stand. My father had made so little of them and beat them down on a constant basis with mental and emotional abuse, they didn't have the strength to take him on. He was far too clever for them and always had an answer to justify his behaviour.

Stranger in the dark...
I got a weekend job in a local clothes shop and how I enjoyed it. Not only did it benefit me financially but I was also meeting new people.

Some weekends my friends would invite me out but the problem was never going out; but on my return. I tried my best to arrive home as late as I could. I would get a lift to our front gate and walk up the lane to the house. This would avoid car noise over the metal grid and headlights shining on the windows of the house. I would tip-toe up to my bedroom and be very quiet but my uncles and father would still complain.

I tried my best when I arrived home late, as I would get a lift to the gate and walk up the lane to the house. This would avoid car noise over the metal grid and headlights shining on the windows of the house.

One night, in the middle of winter I got a lift home. I got out of the car at the gate and walked close to the wall until I got over the metal grid. The night was pitch black, not a star was in the sky. I stood at the gate and gave my eyes a chance to adjust to the blackness that lay before me.

I knew the avenue well so I knew if I took my time I would get home. I started walking slowly, choosing my footsteps carefully. In the distance I heard shuffling footsteps. I kept walking, the footsteps came closer and moved slowly behind me outside the wooden fence. At this point I could hear breathing as well. As the night was pitch black I could see nothing and was too frightened to look behind. All I had on my mind was making sure I got to the back door safely.

Once I made it to the yard, I ran to the back door and closed it behind me putting the bolt safely on. What a relief to be home. I was shaking with fear but couldn't understand who was responsible for the noises, the footsteps and the breathing. I needed to know. I found a torch in the kitchen and went back out.

Opening the bolt on the back door I did think I was mad going back outside, but I wanted to know who was there. I went to the corner of the yard and shone the torch down the side of the avenue where I last heard the footsteps. In the torchlight it was plain to see my worries were no more, before me stood the farm donkey, another pet of mine. He was standing inside the wooden fence and was delighted to get some affection at that hour of the night. I wrapped my arms around his neck in sheer joy and relief that it was him who had followed me home.

Boy trouble...
Every week I looked in the local papers for a job. I desperately wanted to get full-time work so I could get away and make a life

of my own. One week I applied for a job in a local factory doing quality control. I had the interview and got the job. I knew the boss owned flats in the town so I asked him if he had any vacant. He said he had one coming up in the next few weeks and would give me first refusal on it so I was thrilled; life was coming good.

I bought a bicycle and cycled to work every morning. Soon the flat was vacant and I went to see it. It was perfect and was only a five minute walk from work. I set up home in the flat. Finally I was free; from the rows and dysfunction, free to make my own life choices. I cycled home most weekends and if things were really bad I would stay for just a few minutes and return to my little flat in peace. Life was so much better. I was able to get sleep every night with no tension or fights over alcohol and money. Best of all there was no fear, I was safe and secure in my own place now.

I started dating Robert who became very controlling. He was a farmer, a nice guy, but he wanted to know my every move, where I was going and who I was with. I started to feel this was not a good relationship for me so I told him I needed some space to think about my future. He wasn't happy about this and used to arrive unannounced to visit me.

One night I was out with friends and when I came back and opened the door to the complex, the bulb had blown in the light outside my door. I climbed the three flights of stairs and could see in the dim light, someone sitting outside my flat. It startled me as I knew no one should have been in the complex, only those who had a key.

He spoke my name and I knew by his voice it was Robert. I asked him to leave but for weeks afterwards, he would park his car on a side road near the flat. I would look out of my bedroom window and see the front bumper of his car peeping out. This stalking started to freak me out. I became scared of his sneaky behaviour and he started to quote the Bible to me out of context. I needed to get out of the relationship as I felt it was not healthy for me. He started buying me lots of gifts and sending them in the post. It made me angry that he thought he could buy my love.

I remember visiting his home in Limerick where he lived on a farm with his aunt. He had moved into her house when her husband had died and was being given the farm. She told me one day we were alone that he was treating her very badly. I didn't want to get involved as God knows I had enough going on in my own family to deal with. I had made my decision to end the relationship but he would not take no for an answer. He told me I was hanging around with the wrong people and they were a very bad influence on me. I had good friends and went out and about with them, he had no right to pass judgement on people he knew nothing about. Eventually I managed to end the relationship. He would hang around my flat and hound me to talk to him but I told him it was over.

Chapter Ten

MY HUSBAND

I moved on in my life and started going out with a man called John, who would become my husband. I knew his family and we always got along really well. His parents were Irish but had spent many years in England before moving back to Ireland.

The words of a lady I knew as a child came back to me. She lived with her husband down the road from my childhood home. They were English and had come to Ireland when they retired. She was always sewing and doing embroidery and we would sit together and chat the odd time I was allowed to visit her. We spoke about everything from boyfriends to weather. She gave me one piece of advice. She had lived for a few years in Ireland and most of the Irish men she met she did not like, said they treated their wives very badly. Her advice to me was not to marry an Irishman but find a good Englishman. We laughed about it, but it was words I never forgot and time would tell.

I was very happy in my new relationship. John was full of heart, was caring, respectful and of course, handsome. I didn't tell him anything about my past. It was too painful to drag up, it was now in the past and that is where I would leave it, for now anyway.

His parents and family always made me very welcome in their home, many weeks I was invited for Sunday dinner. It was not a dynamic I was used to, the love in the family was very clear to see. I remember one day John's mother came up behind him and wrapped her arms around his waist. She was a tiny woman compared to his six-foot frame. This action freaked me out - in my family I had never received any act of affection, it was alien behaviour to me.

Memories of standing at my granny's grave sobbing my heart out, sad and alone came flooding back. Being scolded to stop crying and pull myself together, no reassurance or comfort given by my family. At no time did I feel loved, cared for or valued in my own family unit and now I was faced with the complete opposite. It felt right for a mother to show love for her son and she did the same with the rest of her family too.

She was a great cook and would always give me a goody bag when I left to go back to my flat on a Sunday evening. I was learning this was the way my life should have been but because of choices my father made, he destroyed my whole family. The dysfunction that lay behind my family's closed doors was toxic and rotten and it would never change as long as my father was drinking. Somehow I knew it would be his life.

I knew in time my brother was coming home to inherit the farms after his army career. I knew I would have to make my own way in life and was thankful I had a job and a good life.

As long as I had the ability to work and look after myself I would never have to face the prospect of returning back to that place that was called home. I often wished I could have erased my past from my mind, it would have made my life a lot easier to be able to forget the pain.

Gone forever...
My mother got very ill in 1981. She had several mini strokes which left her unable to speak. I did visit her and it was hard to see her so unwell.

The last time I went to see her was when John and I got engaged. She was in a nursing home in Dublin and was lying in bed in a darkened room. She looked so different now, her face had changed because of the strokes she had. She looked at us both and I spoke to her. She was unable to utter a word. I told her we had got engaged and I placed her hand on my ring. Tears streamed down her face as if she understood, I hoped they were tears of joy for me.

When I left her that day I was upset as I could see my mother was very unwell. Was I going to lose her now, just when I was making plans for my life? I knew deep within that she was not going to recover again.

She passed away the following year at only 53 years of age. My father arranged for her remains to be brought back to the family plot for burial. I was heartbroken. I always had it in my heart that some day I would be in a position to give her a better life but it was not to be; my mother was gone forever.

Knowing what I know now, I wonder would she have wanted to be brought back to be buried in the family plot. The family that had treated her so badly in life was putting on the public show pretending that she was cared for. My father just wanted to make himself look good. I had lost my mother.

Our wedding day...
The house we built was only five miles from my original home place and with us also building the farm; we thought it was wise to have a small wedding with close friends and family. But my father had other ideas. He insisted on having a big wedding, inviting his friends and people he wanted to impress. He wanted to be seen to be having the big day for his only daughter. Most of the guests that attended I had never met before or would I meet again. I was worried where he was getting the money from to pay for this big wedding he wanted. I asked him about the cost and all he would say was that it was not my concern. I wondered was he taking out a loan against the farm and leave my uncles to pay for it?

I had been saving and had gathered enough money to pay for the wedding dresses and suits. Our flowers had been given as a wedding present, as was the wedding cake. I just had to pay to have it iced.

Making the plans for our wedding was exciting and fun. I was really looking forward to our wedding day but was worried my father would get so drunk he would not be able to walk me down the aisle. I did not want to be given away by a father who was stinking of whiskey, I didn't want him to let himself down on that special day. He had done that so many times before but this was one day I needed him to be there for me.

The morning of our wedding was overcast even though it was August. As I busied myself getting ready a gift arrived for me. My future mother-in-law had sent a present to me and a card welcoming me into the family. It was an antique-gold horseshoe brooch, something I still treasure to this day.

As I was ready to leave the sun burst through the clouds and if that was not enough. My father arrived to collect me and he was sober. During the whole wedding he stayed sober. Was it possible that my life was changing for the better?

It was daylight when we left the hotel, leaving the sound of the band music behind us. In my hand I carried my wedding bouquet. It was a beautiful bouquet filled with freesias, roses and ivy made by a friend of the family. I wanted to take it to my mother's grave.

My mother was laid to rest in a quiet country graveyard just half an hour's drive away. It was a beautiful summer evening. I wondered would my mother have come to our wedding if she was still alive or would my father have kept her away? I remember when I made my confirmation years before she told me in a letter she would come but never turned up, she never told me why. Perhaps my father told her she was not welcome. But today I would leave my wedding bouquet on her grave.

We entered the graveyard through the heavy, black gate. The church had not been in use for many years and was now a ruin as the roof was removed. The windows had also been removed to another church. I remember once going to that church one sunny Sunday morning with my uncle. I remembered the beautiful stained-glass windows lit by the sunlight filtering through the glass. Birds were singing in the trees and the evening sun shone on us both as we walked to my mother's grave. The smell of the flowers from my bouquet drifted into the evening air along with the smell of freshly-cut grass from a field beside the graveyard.

I gently placed the flowers on her grave, saddened by the fact that she was gone from my life. I said a little prayer hoping that if she was in Heaven she was looking down on our day. My husband placed his arm around me. Smiling at each other we were looking forward to the future we would have together.

Chapter Eleven

Married Life

We settled well into married life. We lived in a mobile home and were planning in the future to build a house. We were living on a farm which belonged to John's cousin, for which we paid rent every year, on the understanding that we would inherit it one day. He was a true gentleman. He was crippled with pains and aches but was always in good form. My mother-in-law would drop in to see him every day and bring him meals or if she was away we would do it. Our mobile home was across the yard from his door so it gave him some security knowing that he was not alone.

In the summer he would leave his kitchen door open. The smell of the turf fire in the hearth would waft out into the warm air. He loved nature and the garden so I would often bring him flowers that I grew and place them in a vase on his dresser. One day I pulled gladioli from the garden, they were in full-bloom and I reckoned I had enough for the both of us. Walking from the garden I admired the beautiful array of colours. I took the large bunch into the old man and his eyes lit up in amazement and delight. He told me where he had a big jug that would hold them all. I laughed to myself thinking none of them were going to end up in my home but I didn't have the heart to tell him we would divide the bunch between us. I arranged them in the jug and left empty-handed, disappointed I had none but having such delight in seeing his joy that it did not matter.

The loss of my inheritance...

I went to see the man who was renting my father's shop premises that my parents started their married life in all those years ago. He was serving a customer so as I waited I looked around, it was now a hardware shop. When he was finished I asked him if I could have a word in private. We went upstairs, the living area was just over the shop. As I followed his footsteps I did think if everything had of worked out in my life, this place should have been my home. It was the place my grandfather had given my parents on their marriage. We went into the sitting room and sat down and I told him the reason for my visit.

I explained to him that we had wanted a small wedding with our friends and close relations but my father wanted a big public show. I told him that I was worried where the money was coming from to pay for this big wedding but that my father would not tell me when I asked him about it. I told him about speaking to a friend of his who told me my father had sold the shop a few months before and that's where the money was coming from.

He was quiet and seemed a little uneasy. He told me this was correct; the shop had been sold by my father six months ago. He was surprised that I did not know. I was shocked. Why did my father not tell me? His drinking had been the reason he moved out of the shop in the first place, he had spent his years spending other people's money and now he had access to a lot of cash.

The man went on to say he had been encouraging my father to invest the money wisely but was concerned my father would not do this. He told me it was a shame I didn't have five thousand people at my wedding as that would have used up a lot of the money rather than it being wasted. I left that day feeling angry with my father. Why did I have to hear this news from a stranger? Was my father embarrassed that he was selling what was my true home? It was understood my brother would inherit the farms from my uncles. So I, as his daughter would get nothing. I felt hurt that my father had not told me he had done this. I had hoped that my father would try and keep the shop, to pass on to me. But now it, and the home I spent my first years in, were gone and I knew in my heart, my father would not handle the money from the sale well. It would be used to fund his drinking.

My promised savings...

About a year after we got married we applied for planning permission to build a home. We wanted a bungalow.

As my father would have had the savings from the sale of the shop I felt it was a good time to approach him for the money he had promised me. When I visited him and told him John and I were wanting to get a mortgage and could he help. He just went quiet. I reminded him about the savings book he had promised me. But he just rose from the chair and went upstairs. He entered his bedroom and unlocked the wardrobe removing a brown envelope. On his return to the kitchen he handed it to me. With the smell of whiskey on his breath I felt the safest thing was to thank him and leave.

I drove to the bottom of the steep driveway, turned off the engine and tore open the envelope. Inside was a building society book, the edges of which were shabby and worn. My hands were shaking; I did not know what to expect. I slowly opened the pages. Looking through it, I could see money was put in and taken out again, lots of transactions on each page. I slowly turned to the final page and glanced to the last written line. Tears started to flow as the last line had nothing only noughts written on it. How could he do this to his only daughter? Over the years he had taken money from me promising he was going to help me out in the future to get a home and now after all his promises his help to me was a savings book of zeros.

He had sold the shop for a good price. How could he hand his only daughter a book with nothing in it? I trusted him to do what he said he would. It was made clear to me that in the future my brother would inherit the farms my uncles owned. Was I just been cast out with nothing? He thought nothing of robbing from my uncles over the years so really, why would he worry about robbing from his daughter?

After a few weeks I got the courage up to go back and question him over handing me a worthless account book. I needed to pick a moment when he was sober. I was very hurt that he had done this, but I needed to let him see I was strong and didn't want to break down in front of him. I deserved better and I knew it was his issue that had upset me so much. I felt in my father's eyes, I was worthless. He had put me in that place, many times he had called me many names but how could he claim to have a happy life when he was the cause of so much pain in our family? Was it the only way he could survive, to turn the abnormal into the normal?

I faced him with why he handed me an empty book. He told me about the cost of everything and how he needed the money. He had made me a promise and like all the other promises, he had broken it. I told him that we were very short of money and were trying to get started in life. I knew he had money from the sale of the shop so I felt I was entitled to get back what he stole from me at least. He pulled a cheque book from his pocket. I could tell he was angry with me; I stood near the door so I could do a runner if I needed to get away from him.

He opened the book and wrote a cheque. His writing style was fast and furious. He knew he had wronged me and had no defence. If I hadn't had the courage to ask, he would have got away with what he did. He tore the cheque out of the book at speed. He folded it in two and handed it to me, I thanked him and left. I did not look at it in front of him. I needed to get away. It could have been a blank cheque but I would find out later. I got into my car and drove for home. I had a quick glance at the cheque. It wasn't a very big one but it would help us out with a few bits.

I was glad I had confronted my father for what was rightfully mine. The amount didn't matter but I had won my battle to be valued as his daughter.

Chapter Twelve

The Golden Poison

My father was never far away from a bottle of whiskey. That golden liquid ruled his life in a destructive way and the wave moved through the family like a poison. It would never get a hold of my life because I would stand strong against it. Those in my life who loved me deserved better.

By this time my uncles' farms were very poorly stocked, animals were sold and not replaced. It was hard to see my uncles living a very difficult life with my father bullying them to make sure he had full control of the finances but this situation was out of my control.

One Saturday I arrived on the farm with my tin of buns under my arm. My uncles were finishing their dinner in the dining room, my father was still in bed sleeping off a hangover. I could tell they were in bad form, they looked weary from the life they were living. A cup of tea was poured for me so I sat in and spoke with them. The replies to me were short and curt but again this was not unusual. I offered my uncles a bun from my tin. Uncle James took one but uncle David refused. He went on to say my cooking was terrible and added his usual comment of, *'it would poison a bull'*. He said he couldn't eat it. This had always been his way but today I would teach him a lesson.

He had never given me a compliment in his life and as for my cooking, he would complain about it but as soon as my back was turned he would eat to his heart's content but never let on a word.

Today was going to be different. I put the lid on the tin. Put it down on the table beside me and said I would bring them back home as my husband loved my baking. My uncle was speechless, I knew he did not expect this reaction. I smiled to myself as I knew when I left with my buns he could not munch away behind my back as he normally did.

For many weeks after, I never brought them any cooking but his lesson was not finished. Winter was closing in and I knew they were probably often cold and hungry, so again, I returned with my tin under my arm. I left it on the dining room table. The men were out on the farm but on their return they would see I had brought my tin up again. I wondered what would happen. A week later I returned again. My uncle handed me my tin, it was empty. He very sheepishly said they were grand buns. I smiled to myself, I had taught him a lesson. He was finished insulting and putting me down, it would never happen again.

I felt so sorry for my uncles trapped in this place now and I needed to let them know, despite the past I would always be there for them. A few times when my father was sober I would bring him to town. We would go for some lunch or just a cup of coffee. Soon it was clear the whiskey would steal him away. Many days we would go to town and he would meet one of his drinking buddies and I would be left standing on the side of the street - he would be gone.

None of my business...
On one occasion while driving my father to town he admitted that he had taken money from my uncle's wardrobe. He told me because I had been tidying the wardrobe earlier that day and he was afraid I would be accused of stealing it by my uncle. I thought it was very noble of him to tell me so I wouldn't take the blame for what he had done, but was horrified to see how easy theft was for him. I was also quite sure that it wasn't the first time he had done it.

Later that day I spoke to my uncle about it and asked him to hide his money better but as usual, he told me it was none of my business. After this, any time they would complain to me about my father's drinking, I made it clear that if he had easy access to money he would buy whiskey with it.

As my uncles got older their health suffered. Uncle David, who was always unkind to me, had to have a hip replacement. I told him he could come to our home for a while to recover after his operation. I felt it was the right thing to do even though, over the years he never had a kind word to say to me but I felt that was his problem, not mine. I would look after him and do my bit. He was very humble in our home, very thankful for everything we did for him. I was happy to see his attitude changing and was sad for him, as he must have felt very bad for his behaviour to me in the past and all I was doing was being kind to him in his hour of need.

One day I returned from town. He was sitting in front of the open fire in the sitting room. The wind was howling outside and it was raining; I hoped he was thankful he was enjoying the comfort and peace in our home. No drinking, no rows, only warmth and care.

He said he had something to tell me, so I sat down on a chair beside him. He was looking into the flames of the fire and I waited for him to speak. He thanked me for looking after him and said he wanted to sign his farm over to us - I was totally taken back. He had always been so hurtful and nasty to me and now he wanted to give us his farm. Had the guilt of his bad behaviour hit him, when all he had received from me was kindness? I told him I was not looking after him to get anything; I was doing it because I wanted to.

There was always an understanding when my brother retired from the army he would take on the two farms that my uncles owned, the two farms were side by side. I went on to tell him we were okay. We had a business and a farm, we had enough and so as not to split up the farms it was best to leave them both to my brother.

In some ways I thought I was mad to refuse his offer but no

matter what I felt, I was doing the right thing. I was doing my bit because I cared for him, not for personal gain. I was happy in my life and I would never grab all I could get. I had my own pride and my self respect was far more important than financial gain.

Two weeks passed and my brother arrived down to our home demanding my uncle return to his home. I told my brother it was no problem for my uncle to stay for another while, as he was still very stiff and in pain. I knew his home was cold and damp and not a good place for him to be especially as it was the middle of winter. He was happy with us and had his little chores to do every day so he felt that he was helping us out. My brother was having none of it, he told him to go home.

My uncle David left that day very sad. I felt my brother was very cruel to him but I did wonder if he was worried I would try and take his farm from under his nose. Was that why he wanted David out of our house that day? Was he worried he would lose out if he left David with us? I knew whatever happened, my conscience was clear. I had done the honourable thing and showed care and compassion towards my uncle. I could do no more.

Chapter Thirteen

THE REAL TRUTH

We had a business that provided help for people in their homes. It was hard setting up the farm and money was tight so it was perfect when the business got going.

One day I got a phone call from a lady who needed help with her home. I did not know the lady but got directions to her home and arranged a suitable time to call. I arrived at her door and pressed the bell. A lady came and I explained I had come to help. She looked at me and tears filled her eyes and ran down her face. I asked her was she okay and she told me to come in.

I followed her into a small kitchen and she put the kettle on. She went on to tell me she used to have a good friend years ago who had left town, and I was the image of her. I told her who I was and I realised the woman she spoke of was my mother. I had a lump in my throat; I was worried about what she might tell me. Did I even want to know? She went on to say my mother had a very hard life at the hands of my father. That was all she said, but it was enough to sow a seed. I was confused. This total stranger was telling me a different story to the one my father wanted me to believe.

Her words, her reaction to me at the door, made me sick to my core. My mother was dead and gone, nothing I could do now could put things right. If her words were true how could I face my father again?

As the weeks went by, I was busy getting on with my life. Something niggled away at the back of my mind every day. I thought back to my own childhood: the drinking, the neglect, the constant rows, the mental abuse. Could the words I heard be true? I couldn't hand on heart say they were untrue so I needed to find out for myself. I needed to go and speak to the people who knew my parents while they were married and I needed to find someone I could trust to tell me the truth. I needed to find out the truth.

I went to see a lady I knew very well. She lived across the road from my parents' shop and I always got on well with her. I explained the reason for my visit, she sat and listened then started to cry. She said she had never spoken of my mother because she wanted to protect me from the truth.

What I heard that day shocked me to the core. She told me that my mother was very kind, gentle, softly spoken woman. My father, with his drinking and abuse towards her, had driven her out of our lives. She spoke of terrible fights between them over my father's drinking and abuse.

She told me about being in the shop one day when my father drunkenly lashed out and hit my mother across the face in a violent temper. She spoke of my mother's father coming to stay with them for a while, as he was very worried about the situation. She looked out of her window one morning to see him standing at the shop door and my father throwing his belongings down on the pavement from an open window two floors up. They were shouting at each other but she could not hear what they were saying.

She went on to tell me that when my mother was forced to live in the country with my father's family, she was deeply unhappy and had no life of her own. She was not welcome in that place, no more than I had been. She just existed, trapped in a place of deep torment, abuse and pain.

She told me that one day my mother got a lift home from town with a friend. She had bags of groceries with her. When she arrived at the gate my father was standing there drunk and waving a stick in his hand. He was angry and told her she was not welcome there anymore. He told her she was an unfit mother and waved the stick in her face.

For the first time I realised more what my mother had went through with my father drinking heavily and no doubt she was getting the fallout, not only from him but from my uncles as well. They had done that to me over the years, taking out their anger over his drinking on me, so chances are they were treating her no different. They never spoke her name either so she was of no value in their eyes.

The man who had given her a lift home brought her back into town. How could he leave her in that place? Her life could have been in danger. He dropped her off at her friend's house where she stayed for a few days. God only knows what my mother went through in those days. Who could she turn to for help? There was no social welfare and the attitude at that time was, when married, you had made your own bed, so you should lay in it.

She had lost what should have been her home because of my father's drinking. Being forced to live with his family and now being forced out, with nowhere to go. Torn away from her children and no support to help her out. From her friend's house she left on a train to Dublin and never returned.

I was shocked to hear this. Growing up, my father had always told me my mother left because she was useless and didn't care for us. Somehow things were now slowly making sense. Had he deliberately poisoned us against her so we would never find out the truth of what really happened? She was never part of our childhood but now it made sense to me - she was driven out of our life with abuse - mental and physical.

To the outside world, my father was a saint and could use his charm and wit to his full advantage. It was now making sense to me, how my father had kept us isolated from people and controlled our lives. She also told me that as a baby I had been very sick. I had a bad bout of gastroenteritis and was so ill I was christened in the hospital. Maybe that was the reason I didn't have a godmother, because I was christened in the hospital.

Nowhere to call home...

Many years later, I found out that when my mother went to Dublin she stayed in a hostel as she had nowhere else to go. She arrived at the hostel with nothing, only a small case of clothes and a photo of her two children. Soon after, she suffered a mental breakdown.

How could I forgive my father for what he had done? He was hale and hearty and she was dead. He had destroyed my mother's life with his drinking as he had destroyed my childhood. I was thankful however that I did find out the truth.

Over the years I had resented my mother because of the seeds that were planted in my head and now I knew different. My father had played the victim so well, deserted by his wife to rear his two children. My mother did not deserve the life he gave her. If that happened today, I would like to think she would have had more rights and could have taken care of her children. I am sure she did not want to leave her children with a drunken, abusive father. What choice did she have? None.

Time for healing...

I tried to make peace with my past: the lies, the abuse, neglect and pain. It was not easy. I kept in contact with my family and didn't discuss what I found out with my brother. He always blamed our mother over the years for walking out on us and he was not an easy man to talk to. If I ever spoke to him about anything he didn't want to hear, he would just walk away so I felt there was little point in telling him what I had found out.

I felt it was best to get on with my life and do my own healing.

My brother retired from the army and came home to take over the running of our uncles' farms which were signed over to him. I visited on occasion but nothing had changed. My father was still drinking heavily, still taking money from my uncles and drinking the money he had got from the sale of his shop. I got on with my life. I was busy with our business and doing well.

I went to see my father's doctor one day, concerned about his health and future. He told me there was nothing he could do to help our father unless he wanted to get help himself; it was not the words I wanted to hear.

Over the years' numerous people had tried to help my father come off the drink. The local clergy used to visit and my father would always be present. Thy would encourage my father to cut back on his drinking but he never listened. The wife of the schoolmaster who often used to share his lunch with me, told me years later, that she often spoke with my father about his drinking and being responsible for two children. I am sure many people spoke to him about his drinking but he ignored them.

Chapter Fourteen

Rescuing Uncle James

One day on a visit back home, my father was very drunk. He was standing in the kitchen with his hands in a plastic basin of hot water, washing the dishes.

My uncle David was sitting in a chair just staring into the flames of the open fire, not acknowledging the fact that I had just arrived. He never spoke a word and I could tell by my father's mood, things were not good.

He was lifting plates out of the basin and throwing them very roughly into the rack to drain. I often thought it was a miracle there was any delph left in the house at all. My father did not take much care of what he was doing, especially under the influence of whiskey. Plates and cups often had cracks and were badly chipped. I wondered that day if I had disturbed a row between them or was it just the usual of my father shouting abuse and my uncle just staying quiet for the sake of peace.

My father told me in his drunken voice that my uncle James, was up in bed and was sick. He spoke abruptly to me and using curse words he basically said: "I am not going to look after him."

It did not surprise me to hear these words coming from my father's mouth as on so many occasions before, I had listened to his rage and nasty words. I never answered him. I could see the anger rising in him and didn't fancy having some crockery or cutlery flying in my direction, so I just quietly left the kitchen and went upstairs to my uncle's bedroom. It was a large room with the vinyl floor covering well worn and from the windows hung net curtains that had seen better days; they were full of holes and spots of green mould from the damp.

It was winter and his room was cold, I could see my warm breath in the air. Uncle James lay in his bed crouched in a fetal position, shaking like a leaf and his eyes were not focused. I was shocked. He was covered in a light, cotton sheet. I spoke to him and asked how he was but he was barely able to speak to me. I grabbed a blanket from the floor beside his bed and gently spread it over him. The weight of the blanket caused him to cringe in pain.

I went back downstairs to the kitchen and asked where my brother was. He was the man of the house so I thought it was best to talk to him to see if he had spoken to a doctor. My father answered me with a string of abuse. I went outside looking to find my brother.

Near the house was a shed called the thrasher shed. It housed machines from a bygone era. I went out past the shed and at the top of my voice called my brother's name. He answered me from a field behind the shed a short distance away. As he walked towards me, I knew I had to stay calm. I was livid to see my uncle being left to suffer the way he was but maybe there was an explanation, maybe a doctor had been called and was on his way.

When he got to where I stood, I calmly asked him if he had called a doctor for our uncle? His reply was one I have never, or will ever forget, and made my blood run cold. With a cold, hard look in his eyes his reply to me was: "How can I bring a doctor around here with the state of the place?" I was horrified and saddened that my brother would treat our uncle in this manner. He had inherited his farm from him but was out walking the fields and leaving our uncle to suffer. I left that day with a heavy heart after telling him to contact the doctor.

I returned early next morning. My father was still in bed and my other uncle, David was sitting in the kitchen. He told me how my brother had taken my uncle from his bed in severe pain, put him in his car and taken him to the doctor. I felt relieved but also saddened that he would not call a doctor to the house as it would have been easier for my uncle. The doctor sent him straight to hospital where he recovered well but was very frail. I felt I had to do something to safeguard him against going back to the home he had come from. Winter was setting in and with his failing health how could I let him be sent home again? All sorts of things went through my mind. Had my brother got what he wanted? He had our uncle's farm in his name now so was my uncle of no further use? I always tried to think the best of my brother but after what had happened, I worried about the future for both of my uncles.

My father had always spoken down to them called them, idiots and fools, made little of them every chance he got. I felt the best thing to do was to go and speak with my uncle's doctor before he was discharged and voice my concerns.

On hearing my story, the doctor agreed not to send him home but to send him to a nursing home. Uncle James was very upset about this. I spent an afternoon with him in the hospital listening to him crying and giving out about the man my father was. It broke my heart to see him upset because if home life was normal family life, he could have gone home.

He was always a very quiet and gentle man, I always had a high regard for him. He was the eldest uncle and the house was his. He allowed me to live in his house and eat from his table. We didn't always see eye-to-eye, I remember he wouldn't come shopping with me when I was a little girl, but I never lost sight of the fact he was also a victim of my father's alcoholism.

He moved into a nursing home and took a long time to settle in. Visits to him were hard but he blossomed with the care he was getting at the home. I felt happy in the knowledge he was safe and at least now he was being looked after.

Time for change...

I kept up visits with my other uncle and brother but nothing had changed; my father was still behaving as usual. Because I could keep the visits short and drive away, I could cope.

It was hard to leave my uncle David living with my father, but I hoped my brother would keep an eye out for him. My brother would constantly complain to me about the nursing home James was in. It was too far away and he didn't like the place. Nothing about how well he now was because he had nursing home care, just complaint after complaint. I just learned to let it go over my head. I was so thankful I could drive away to a happy loving home shared with my husband.

One day I went back to visit. It was spring and buds were on the trees. Snowdrops and crocuses were starting to appear to give their show of colour, the front lawn at the house was covered in little green shoots just waiting to spring forth. I went into the kitchen; all was quiet and I presumed my brother had taken my father to town as my brother's car was not in its usual place. David was sitting in his chair in front of the fire. His head was bowed and I knew something was wrong. I asked him if he was okay and he said he wasn't. He went on to say he wanted to leave the house, he could not stay there any longer.

What I saw that day was a sad, old frail man. No longer was he the man who could kick the dog for the sake of it, hold me to a electric fence for the fun of it, or throw verbal abuse at me. He was alone and broken and now desperate for me to help him. I knew it was pointless speaking with my brother, I had seen the nasty side of him when dealing with my other uncle. He would probably deny anything was wrong, just to leave him at home.

Uncle David went on to tell me my father was being very nasty to him. He was drinking every day and he was dealing with the consequences of that. He said he had spoken to my brother about it but he would not listen. My father was throwing his food out to the dog, he was unable to have a meal for himself. I was so sorry for him; I knew something had to be done. He desperately wanted to leave. I asked him if he would be happy to go to a nursing home where he could have company all day.

I felt coming to us was not an option as my brother wouldn't let him stay and we were both out working all day, so he would be totally on his own. He wanted to go to a nursing home, anywhere. He was desperate. I left him and told him I would return later. I rang the Health Board who knew of him already as the year before he had been assessed. I spoke to a lady and explained what was going on. She said if I found him a bed in a nursing home the Health Board would cover the costs. She too, felt it was better he left the house.

I rang a nursing home a few miles away, which was run by a lady I knew, and it was very homely. She had a bed available and told me he was very welcome. I returned to my uncle that evening. The daylight was fading fast and the kitchen was dark. A few red embers sat in the open hearth. I told him I had found a place for him to go, he was happy with that. This decision had to be his. He lifted himself from the chair, I knew we needed to get out before my father and brother returned. He was stiff with pains and aching joints and it was an effort for him to walk. He turned and faced the door and without uttering a word slowly began to walk to the back door. I felt his pain as I had felt my other uncle's pain.

These two men were being driven from their home by my father's behaviour. My uncle got into my car and we drove to the home. I told him I would sort clothes for him the next day but for now he needed to get to a place where he felt safe and not threatened.

That night I thought of my mother doing the very same thing years before because of my father's drinking; he had forced her out and now he was doing the same thing to his brothers. The only difference now, was at least my uncle had me to help him whereas my mother had nobody.

He settled very well in the nursing home and was very happy to be out of the house, away from my father. On my visits to see him he would often mention my brother was not happy that he was no longer at home. My uncle was unable to do very much, crippled with pain in his joints. My brother kept hounding him and one day when I visited he was convinced he would have to go home. He felt he had no choice because of the pressure my brother was putting on him. I spoke to him and told him if he was happier to stay where he was, that is what he should do. He had not had an easy life and was enjoying the comfort and care that he now had. Surely he was now entitled to some peace and contentment in his old age? I spoke with my brother about leaving him in peace but he just walked away. I was beginning to think my brother was getting very like our father. Everything in life was his way or no way. Other people's needs or feelings didn't come into it.

Chapter Fifteen

FAMILY TROUBLES

One day I got a phone call from the Health Board to say they were moving my uncle James to another nursing home from the one he was in. It suited very well as it was closer to home. The reason they gave me for wanting to move him was cost. The nursing home he was in was a private one and the cost of his care was a lot higher than the one he was moving too. It was ideal as it meant my uncle would have a surplus from his pension, which was something he never had.

I helped him get settled into the new home. He was a lot happier to be back nearer home. I kept charge of his account and as his little surplus started to build I would let him know that if he needed anything, he now had his own money to pay for it. Visiting him was a pleasure, he was happy and getting the care he needed.

My brother was often in contact by phone complaining about our father's behaviour, especially his drunkenness, him falling around the house every night, not arriving home till early morning many times. Often his clothes would be dirty and torn as he had spent the night lying in a ditch. I knew in the past my brother had given my father access to his bank accounts. On one occasion my brother let him take charge of his pay cheques on one of his overseas visits, to be lodged into his bank account. On my brother's return, he discovered my father had cashed all his cheques and his bank account was empty. I knew he was taking my father to visit his drinking friends, then complaining to me when my father would come home drunk. My brother was also now part of the problem. I'm sure the money from the shop was long gone.

My brother rang me one day and complained that our uncles' clothes were not suitable, complaining I had their pension books. I then took the step of handing in their pension books to the nursing homes. I felt it was the best way forward and if my uncles needed anything the nursing home could get it for them. Uncle James had a surplus of several thousand in an account. I closed the account and sent the cheque to my brother. If he wasn't happy with their clothes he could now sort it himself. My other uncle was in a private nursing home and all his pension went to pay for his keep. I didn't want conflict with my brother so I felt I was doing the right thing. The most important thing was my uncles were happy and being looked after.

My final visit home...
On my visits home, old memories would come flooding back of my youth. When I was in the house, it was like I could experience the fear and the pain all over again.

Sometimes I thought my father was such a clever man he would have made a great politician and could have supported his family. Meals he cooked for us as children were often awful. Attempting to cook while in a drunken haze was never a good idea. He would use left-over food from days before, throwing all into one pot and cooking it in the oven. As a very small child I got a bad attack of gastroenteritis. Is it any wonder?

I visited the house one dark day in the middle of winter. I got the back door key from its hiding place and unlocked the door. The house was empty. I had no particular thoughts that day, only to go to my uncle's wardrobe to pick up a vest for him that he asked me to get.

As I approached the kitchen from the scullery I could smell the damp and the fire in the grate was smouldering. I stood at the kitchen door unable to move my feet. In the middle of the kitchen I could picture my two uncles fighting with my father over his drinking, then it faded away. The light in the kitchen was dim but the scene was as real as if they were really there. I pulled myself together and told myself this was my mind playing tricks.

I left the kitchen and went to the sitting room; it was a big room that contained a large table with chairs and a sideboard with a large mirror over it.

The sideboard had an array of ornaments and fancy glass caked in dust, plants were growing in pots in the deep windowsill and the room was cold and still stank of stale cigarettes and whiskey. The large table was covered in papers, books, torn envelopes and bills. At one end of the table stood an open half-bottle of whiskey with an empty glass beside it. On the floor, lay my father. He had been sick, wet himself, eyes rolling around in his head and in his hand was an empty glass.

I had often witnessed this sight as a child. What was happening? My father wasn't even in the house that day so why was my mind playing these tricks on me? It was so real. The smell, the sight that lay on the floor in front of me. I quickly left the room and across the corridor was a room with an old piano in it. This was a room with a table and chairs and a long sideboard stacked up with oil lamps, fancy glass and ornaments. The old piano was at the far end of the room. On many days as a child I used to sing and play to myself. The piano was out of tune and so was I, but it felt good.

The walls were covered in paintings and old family photos. Mostly of generations gone before. I opened the door and stood. In the centre of the room, against a chair a little girl was kneeling with head bowed and hands held in prayer. She wore a white, navy and red striped cardigan; a cold shiver ran up my spine as I realised that little girl was me. I prayed a little prayer to God to protect me that day. I had often come to the house when it was empty but I never had an experience like this. I needed to get out and leave the place.

I quickly left the room and went to my uncle's room. I found his vest and quickly left the house. As I locked the door and put the key back in its hiding place a real sense of fear and evil came over me.

Chapter Sixteen

My Fading Father

As my father got older, his drinking continued. My brother used to drive him wherever he wanted to go. He attended funerals all over the country. He smoked heavily all his life and this affected his health so he was in and out of hospital with lung problems. His future was always a worry as he got frailer and age came against him.

One morning my brother rang in a panic - my father needed to go to day care. A neighbour who worked near the centre used to always bring him in, but on this day he was refusing to go with her and was drunk. I went up to the house. The front door was open and as I approached I could hear him talking to himself in the sitting room, just inside the front door. He was sitting in a chair mumbling to himself. Many times over the years he would talk away to himself sometimes giving off to other people, sometimes his words never making any sense, so it was easy for me to ignore his chatter.

He agreed to let me drive him into day care. He stood up with a real effort and seemed very unsteady on his feet. He picked up a large glass of green/yellow coloured liquid and drank it back. I asked him what it was, and did he need to be drinking it? He very quickly told me to mind my own business.

He slowly walked out to my car, mumbling away to himself and got in. I pulled the door behind me and hoped the trip would be okay. Few words were spoken on the short journey. I decided it was wiser for me to remain silent as he had a stick in his hand.

Whatever he had been drinking from the glass before we left had now caused him to be slumped in the seat. I pulled the car up at the front of the day care and went in for help. Finding a small group of care helpers I asked them could they help me with my father. Between us all, we were able to bring him into the day care room. At least he would be safe here.

I drove away that day worried that if he was coming into day care drunk on a regular basis, they would refuse to take him in. He was too hard to manage and also they had the safety of other clients to consider. I went home and rang my brother and told him the story. I agreed to take him into day care the next day too and hoped after that, things would return to normal. When I collected him the next morning - he was sober.

On the journey I did remark about the worries I had, that the daycare would refuse to take him if he continued to turn up in the state he had been in the previous day. Immediately his mood changed and started to bang his stick on the floor; shouting and denying that he had been drunk the previous day.

He said he was fine and I was misinformed. I was fearful he was very angry and I was worried the stick was going to come in my direction. I prayed to God to get me safely to the day care door and vowed I would never put myself in this position again. Denial was his favourite defence. I suppose the only way he could exist in his broken world was to deny everything and always blame someone else. It was always someone else's fault, never his own.

I was so thankful that day that I no longer lived at home. I was away having my own life, now married to a man who had nothing but respect and love for me and did not need alcohol as a crutch to live his live. I was happy my uncles were away from him as well and getting the care they deserved.

No job too small...
We ran our business for fifteen years. It was a good business, started from my love of sewing. I had no formal training and from a very small start it snowballed into a good business. I was happy. I was rising up and doing well for myself, I did not need their approval now. I was now an adult making my own life. My husband was involved too and was very handy with his hands. Learning to fit curtains came easy to him. I was very proud, not in a boastful way but pleased that we had achieved a good business through hard work.

Through the business I met a lot of people. Some of them became friends and are still our friends today. I worked very long hours and enjoyed it all. We did everything from a cottage to a castle. No job too big or too small.

Over the years I suffered with bad sinusitis. As the years went by I lived with continual headaches, a blocked nose and constant ear infections. As time went on my health was getting worse. I also over the years had problems with my feet and had to wear specially-made insoles so I could walk without pain.

A foot specialist had told me years before that someday, I would be facing major surgery as my feet had been destroyed from the footwear I wore as a child and as a teenager from wearing shoes that were way too small for my feet. My feet had been crushed up and not allowed to grow properly. As time went on, it would cause major problems in the metatarsal bones in both my feet. I did my best and worked away.

We decided to close the business. It had been our life for many years but with the long hours and heavy work load, we felt there were easier ways to earn our living. We had also been left unpaid from a large job we had done and we ended up going to court to get it sorted. We won our case but found the whole thing very stressful.

We felt if we worked for someone else, life would be easier. It was a very hard decision to make as the business had been such a big part of our lives.

Then I got pneumonia. I will never forget the pain. It travelled to both my lungs. The doctor would not send me to hospital as there was a sickness bug going around the hospital and he felt I would recover better at home.

Years of sinus infection had taken its toll on my health. My husband rang my brother to tell him I was very ill. I expected a visit or a phone call but neither came. I recovered after a few weeks but the sinus was still pulling me down. With so much mucus in my body it was impossible for me to get healthy.

I decided to take a year out to have a break and decide what I'd like to do. A friend was going to study nursing and knew it was something I had often said I would like to do. She asked me to go along and we would train together. My head was so blocked up with mucus all the time, I felt to study for anything would be an impossible task and I was just so tired. I needed to take a break.

A man I knew approached me one day. He had a hardware and giftware shop in the local town and he asked if I would come and work for him - I told him I was taking a year out. I wondered if I was doing the right thing as it was a job offer and may not come my way again. He knew my family well and when I explained I felt I needed to take time off to do things for my uncles and father, he was very understanding. It was strange taking a year off for myself. I had always worked, was always busy, but now it was time for me.

During the time I was off work I decided one day to visit my brother. When I arrived he told me he didn't contact me when I was sick because our father would not let him. I felt disappointed, hurt and angry with him. What a feeble excuse. He was an adult with his own mind. Where was the care or heart for me? But I let it go as I felt there was little point in saying anything. I knew I would probably only be upsetting myself to confront them, as they both had proved to me so many times there was no regard or heart in the family for me.

Chapter Seventeen

OPENING UP ABOUT THE PAST

The months went by very fast. I did a little gardening and spent time at home with our dogs. Our bungalow was my sanctuary. We did a lot of the work ourselves to get it built and finished. It was a happy place with no drinking, no foul moods and no fear within its walls. My husband came from a very stable family and was very understanding about my family situation. I never let him fight my battles for me and he would always praise me highly in the company of my father, any chance he got. He often listened to me for hours about the workings of my dysfunctional family and that was good for my own healing.

We were married for many years before I opened up to my husband and spoke of the pain in my childhood. It was buried deep inside and the words of my father were still in my head, not to carry stories. I thought growing up, my family was normal. I thought it was just life and you did your best and got on with it. No matter what I did for my family, it was never right. I had no value in that place. The value was placed in my brother. He was the eldest son, who was the golden-haired boy. I knew there were serious problems in my family when I saw the relationship my husband had with his family. There was a care and respect for each of the children, and there was love in the home. My mother never had my family's approval and neither did I. Was history repeating itself?

The hatred, pain and abuse that drove my mother away was

driving me away too. My family was toxic and destroyed. I could not change the past or fix my family, I could only focus on my future and build a better life.

Towards the end of my year out, I went to see the man who had offered me a job. I did think that maybe by now he would have employed someone else but he offered me a position, we sorted terms and conditions and I was happy. I would be working part-time for someone else. No longer did I have to keep accounts, pay VAT, work late. It was ideal - I was ready to return to work.

I settled into the job and enjoyed it. My sinus was still bad and I got pneumonia again, however, this time it was not as bad as it was only in one lung. Back on antibiotics again to clear it, I recovered but my system was very weak. I had no energy and was glad I was only working part-time. I had a constant ear infection in one ear and I would pick up a cold very easily. Colds would always turn to a chest infection, antibiotics again to clear the infection. It was a vicious circle but I worked away and did my best.

Visits from my father and brother were rare. Once, they came to the house and my father had a brown paper bag under his arm which he handed to me. I opened it and it contained the diamond shaped picture from his bedroom wall. The frame was now rotten with woodworm but the painting and glass was perfect. He always knew I liked it, as I had told him so many times. Was he giving me this gift now, just to make some type of amends in his own mind? I got it reframed and put it on our sitting room wall.

Christmas was always a hard time. I would ask my brother and father to Christmas dinner and often my father would be too drunk to come and my brother would arrive late. My uncles always preferred to stay at the home. After a few years of trying to do a nice Christmas dinner for them I gave up. I always got frustrated and annoyed at the fact that my father couldn't care less that I was going to the trouble of cooking a nice dinner. It also didn't help when my brother couldn't be bothered to turn up on time. It was very clear that my father preferred to spend time with his drinking buddies,.

A dangerous lifestyle...

One day, a lady I knew well came into the shop. She was pale and withdrawn and I knew by the look on her face, something was wrong. We went to a corner of the shop where it was quiet and she told me that on her way home the night before she met my father on the road. She was a very careful driver and had not been driving fast. She saw a figure staggering along the white line in the middle of the road and getting closer she saw it was my father. Thank God it was her that found him. If it had been a fast driver on the road, the outcome could have been very different.

She pulled in beside him and gave him a lift to his door. She was shaken but felt she should let me know. I decided to do something. He was due into respite care the following week. It was a week away from home in the nursing home attached to the day care centre. At least it was one week I knew he was safe. He would not be staggering home alone, at risk of destroying another family. My husband and I spoke about what we would do and decided the best way forward was to get him into long-term care. The problem was only going to get a lot worse as he got older. We knew this was not going to be easy. He wasn't sick or ill, he was just an alcoholic.

A year before, we had asked the Health Board to assess him. The public health nurse would always let him know a few days before she intended to visit and he would always make sure on these days he was sober and charming. When he was sober he could get around very well, so really he was only a risk to himself or others when he was under the influence of alcohol. She asked him one day, if there was running water and bathing facilities in the house as part of her assessment? He said yes and the box was ticked.

There was a bath yes, but the only source of water to it was a cold tap that was fed from a tank on top of the roof. That water was ice cold, maybe a little warmer in the summer from the heat of the sun. I remember many times having a wash down with cold water in a plastic basin. If I could, I would boil the kettle in the kitchen to add some hot water but if my father was drunk and the mood was bad with my uncles it was easier just to use cold water. That was the washing facilities but the boxes were ticked, so all was well. When she finished her assessment she rang me one day to give me her findings. She said in her opinion, my father was a gentleman. He was fine and she saw no evidence that he had an alcohol problem and that was it.

I went to see her the following day and gave her letters from the local guards, my father's doctor and local curate all voicing the same concerns for his safety and the safety of others. She put them in her file but as far as she was concerned, the case was closed.

A week later I visited my father. I found him unconscious on the sitting room floor, a whiskey bottle sat empty on the table. He was breathing all right but I knew he was probably just after drinking the full bottle of whiskey and this was the result. I rang the public health nurse and asked her could she come or send someone out to see the state he was in. She said the Health Board would not get involved. He had been assessed and that was it.

At that time he was having a lot of falls, ending up with black eyes and torn hands. Asking him what caused the damage, he always had an answer. It was a door opening in the wind, hitting his face or a briar in a ditch, hitting off his hands as he walked by. Deep down I knew this was more denial.

My husband came with me to the nursing home where we asked to see the matron. She was a middle-aged woman, immaculately dressed and well spoken. My husband was a good speaker and knew how to handle situations without anger. I was filled with sinus infection and weary from everything so I let him do the talking.

My husband explained to the matron what had happened on the road and the falls my father was having. He was getting more frail every day. She said there was nothing she could do, as in their opinion there was no medical need. Hang on a minute I thought. All the experts in this field, in my research, tell me alcoholism is a disease. If it is a disease and putting someone's life in danger, surely that is a medical need. But I did not speak. My husband told her in a gentle, persuasive voice it would be sorted before the week was out.

He asked her who he could speak to in the Health Board that would have the authority to get it sorted. My husband explained to her that the responsibility was falling back on me all the time. My brother was to turn up to this meeting and never did. He would duck and dive if a problem had to be sorted and this was no different. The matron said to leave it with her and she would see what she could do.

My father went into respite care the next week and that was the beginning of his nursing home care. I was so relieved. No longer would I worry about him on the road, or falling asleep in his bed with a burning cigarette in his hand and setting the house on fire, or falling into a ditch on a freezing cold night and dying of hypothermia. No longer would I have to listen to my brother complaining about his behaviour, even though I knew my brother was part of the problem. He never put any pressure on my father to contribute to the house from his pension and would give my father access to drink with his buddies. I did think that maybe my brother was not strong enough to stand up to our father. Perhaps had I been in the same position, I would have done the same.

Chapter Eighteen

PROBLEM PAGES

One weekend while looking through the Sunday Independent, I stopped at the problem page. I read through the page and thought I might just write to the paper. If my letter was valid, it would be printed I thought. I wouldn't put my name to it, so no one would know it was me who sent it in and I would change the details slightly just to see what advice they would give. I knew my father wouldn't be happy about me going to a national newspaper but I was curious. I posted my letter in a nearby town and checked the paper every week, just to see if it would be printed.

Then about a month later, I opened the problem page and there was my letter printed as I had written it. That Sunday my brother called to the house, he said someone had written to the newspaper with a problem the same as ours. I kept calm and very quickly concluded I would not tell him that it was me, as he would probably not have been pleased about it. I read the letter as if it was the first time I had seen it and tried to sound surprised. Then I made an excuse in case I would blow my cover and told him we were going out to friends that evening, so he left.

This is the letter as it was printed in the paper...

My dad's lifetime of drink still haunts us!
"I write this letter to you with a shaky hand and a heavy heart. If my father knew I was writing to you he would be extremely angry with me. I am now in my 40's and the

daughter of an alcoholic. As long as I remember he has been a heavy drinker. My mother left him after I was born as she could take no more of his drinking. He then moved in with his sister, taking my brother and me with him. Our childhood was made up of constant rows because of his continued drinking, of regularly finding him passed out from drinking and of regularly having him dragged up legless to our room at night and dumped on the floor and not knowing whether he was dead or alive."

"He has caused so much upset in the family over the years, but to the outside world he is a real charmer. He was always careful to keep us under tight scrutiny when we were young, never letting us go anywhere unless he was with us, and never allowing friends in to play. I now know this was his way of keeping control. He was afraid if we spoke out, it would tarnish his image."

"As I got older I gathered sufficient confidence to go to his doctor to try and get some kind of support. This was a complete waste of time and effort. All my family who were affected by his drinking have taken out their anger on me over the years and I have now had enough. I have confronted my father several times about his drinking, but he is in complete denial. And because of all his verbal abuse and selfishness, I have cut all ties with him."

"I tried in recent months to get him into a nursing home as he is now in his late 70's. We are concerned for his safety and as he staggers home on a main road that he will cause an accident. He also has huge bills in the local shops and loans in local banks which will probably never be paid. We recently discovered he is stealing from my brother to fund his drinking. He will go to any lengths to feed his addiction. We have talked to the health authorities but their attitude is that he is fine and we need counselling. We are at our wits end and don't know where to go from here. At times I think this problem will only be solved when he dies, and I hate myself for thinking that."

One Sunday while reading the problem page in the Sunday World. I came across a letter from a child living in an alcoholic home. Again, I felt compelled to send in a letter to give them hope that life would not always be like that and I was living proof that through good choices, life would get better for them.

I changed some of the details slightly and posted my letter. A few weeks later that letter was printed too. This is what it said...

My drunken dad will ruin our Christmas again!

"I am dreading the festive season this year. Christmas will no doubt be ruined for me because of alcohol. I am one of hundreds of Irish people who dread Christmas for this reason. I myself don't drink but come from a house with an alcoholic parent. A parent we all love when sober but have an absolute abhorrence for when drunk."

"My father's drinking tends to get worse at Christmas but it is something we have come to expect and in a way accept. We have all tried to talk to him but it is like knocking your head off a brick wall. Naturally, as with all alcoholics, he sees nothing wrong."

I always kept a copy of the letters. I was proud of myself for having the courage to write and to see they were good enough to be printed. The shop where I worked was always busy, I enjoyed the job and got on well with the other staff. It suited me so well, my health was not the best but I got on with life. The sinusitis was so draining and the pneumonia had taken its toll on me.

One day a lady I knew came into the shop. She thought I was very pale and asked if I was okay. I told her my health issues and she said her husband had been to see a herbalist for an issue that he had for years which the doctors couldn't help him with. He got very good results with herbal medicine. I thought it wouldn't do me any harm to check it out. There were days I was so bad, especially in the damp days of winter, if someone had told me to stand on my head to ease my problem, I would have tried it. Most days it was a struggle to take a breath and I was getting worse. I was taking more and more antihistamine and getting fewer results.

On visiting the herbalist, he took my life history, he said my body was so full of mucus it was poisoning my system which made sense to me. He agreed he would work with me but said I would have to do as he said, otherwise I would be wasting my money and his time; I agreed.

At this point I felt so unwell with no energy and zest for life and knew I had to take positive action. He put me on a detox of only brown rice, vegetables and fruit, fresh fish and organic chicken. A very healthy diet with only herbal teas and water to drink. He also gave me a bottle of liquid, made up from several herbs. I left his clinic making a promise to myself that I would take his advice, in the hope of better health.

The following weeks were very difficult. As the herbs and detox started to kick in, I felt very unwell. I was told this would happen as mucus cleared from my body; the taste in my mouth was so bad and my stomach felt sick all the time. I became a dab hand at cooking my limited range of food - it was all healthy food so I felt it was doing me good. The amount of mucus that cleared from my head every day was amazing, I often wondered where it was all coming from. It was going to take time for my body to heal but I was determined to stick with it. All the food I was eating was healthy and it was going to make me better. I'd had the problem so long it was going to take time to heal.

Father's rules...
My father stayed put in the nursing home. He was allowed to go out to town every day and he was getting fed and looked after. Many days in the past at home, I wondered if he ever ate. He had to give up his pension book to the nursing home and they would give him back the balance after his bill was paid every week. It was a good idea as the less money he had, the less whiskey he could

buy. They would give him a small drink of whiskey before he went to bed every night and that was to keep his cravings at bay. My brother would buy a bottle of whiskey every week and give it to the nurses to keep for him. I used to drop in on a regular basis. I would bring him cigarettes which is what he asked me for. It was clear on many visits though he was drinking more than the glass of whiskey he was getting at night. He was often short-tempered and snappy and I could smell whiskey on his breath.

Very soon it was made clear to me, my problems with my father were far from over. The nursing home had their rules but he was making his own. Why should this be a surprise to me? He had lived by his own rules all his life. The matron called me to her office. The drinks cabinet was in a little office at the end of a corridor, it was always kept locked and only the staff members had a key. The night before, a nurse had gone to the office to get my father's nightly drink. As she was sorting drink for him and the other patients who required it, my father appeared at the door. He was drunk. The nurse asked him to go to his room but he went over to her and pushed her against the wall and held her there. He complained that the bottle of whiskey was his and he should have it and drink it whenever he wanted. She was frightened but thankfully she managed to get away from him and seek help.

The matron made it clear to me that day, that this behaviour would not be tolerated. He had broken her rules and terrified a staff member. She also told me people were bringing him in whiskey and he was buying it out of his weekly allowance also. I left that day knowing in my heart, this would not be the first and last time the matron would call me into her office.

I spoke to my father about what had happened and he denied it. It wasn't him, must have been someone else. Lying came so easy to him. I stopped bringing him cigarettes as if he had to buy his own, it would give him less money to buy whiskey. He fought with me about this, demanding I buy them complaining about all he had done for me and now I would not even buy him his cigarettes. It was easy for me to walk away from him that day. What had he ever done for me? Neglected me and drove my mother away, destroyed my family with his life choices, sold a property, the balance of the money ending up in the pubs and washed down the toilet. What a waste. The father I had walked away from, I owed him nothing. All he had given me was heartbreak and broken promises.

Chapter Nineteen

Reuniting the Brothers

A new health centre was built and my father and uncle David moved into it, in different rooms. Uncle James was a few miles away in another home. He was happy and contented but costs started to rise where he was. My brother said he would not pay the difference even though it was pittance. He contacted the Health Board and demanded he was to be moved to the same place as my other uncle and father. This upset my uncle James, he did not want to move. He was happy where he was and didn't want to move back to be in the same place as my father. I spoke with my brother about it and as far as he was concerned it wasn't my business. The matron in the home knew my uncle didn't want to leave and said she would prefer him to stay if that is what he wanted. She said she would do her best to keep costs to a minimum. But my brother eventually got his way and soon my two uncles and father were together again.

The matron's office...
Sometimes my brother and I would be called to the matron's office. But most of the times Michael would not come. For instance we got a call one day from the matron and I went to see Michael to collect him. He was with a neighbour placing sheep into a pen. He told me he would not be going as he was to busy.

Maybe that was his way of coping with life. Maybe he was as fed up as I was with the lifetime of problems our father had caused. In the past if we met the matron together, Michael would sit on a chair in the corner and say nothing while she said her piece. The talking was always left to me.

One day a lady came to the shop. She told me she was prepared to take my father out as she knew I wouldn't take him anywhere. I felt it was pointless trying to explain anything to her as it was obvious her mind was made up so I wished her well. A few days later she returned with an apology. She had taken my father to a nearby town where he went drinking with his mates and would not return to the nursing home with her. She now understood why I would not take him out.

My biggest fear now was that my father would be sent home, so I went to see the matron on my own. I was worried about Michael's mental health as he would not communicate with me very much and seemed to be cutting himself off. He would not return calls or messages and if I met him, he did not seem keen to chat. I worried about the effect our father's drinking was having on him. The Health Board offered us both counselling at one point, but Michael laughed mockingly at the idea, saying our father was the one with the problem not us.

That day, the matron had spoken of my father having little respect for staff or residents and she said he was drinking too much. Michael was returning him late to the home after he took him out for the day, often in a drunken state. This behaviour had to stop. She suggested a meeting with our father. I asked her to contact Michael after what had happened before, to get him to come in.

I met my father on the way out that day. He saw me coming out of the matron's office and was very angry because I would not tell him my business with her. I quickly left that day.

The meeting was arranged though I felt in my heart it wouldn't change a thing. My father had lived by his own rules all his life; he was fairly mobile so he could make his own choices. Why should he now follow rules and consider other people? He was getting older, why should he now do what others wanted, at least that was the way he would see it.

We had a meeting a week later, on my way to the home I

wondered if my brother would attend. When I arrived, and walked into the matron's office, there was Michael sitting in his usual place, the chair furthest away. At least he was there, the matron was sitting at her desk, there was an awkwardness in the room, it was quite clear there was little conversation before I arrived. I sat down and she told us that my father, two days before, had gone missing from the home. I was shocked.

He had left in the afternoon and that night never returned when he should have for bed. Late that night they got a phone call from a lady to say she had returned home to her mother's house and found my father drunk in the hallway. Her mother was also an alcoholic. The nursing home staff went and brought my father back to his room and had to leave a nurse with him all night as they were afraid he would fall out of the bed or try and climb out and hurt himself.

The matron made it clear that day, that this could not happen again. He would have to follow the rules while in their care. My brother never spoke, I agreed with her.

My father arrived in and sat down. I wondered what his excuse would be this time, I wondered how he would react to someone telling him he had to follow rules. He always dressed in a suit and a tie, always tried to look smart. It didn't hide the awful smell of stale whiskey and cigarettes and often his clothes would be stained and have an odd cigarette burn. He was all chat about the day and how everybody was keeping.

The matron went on to tell him what she told us minutes before. I could see by his body language he was far from happy with what she was saying. She told him from that day on, he was only going to be allowed out with either myself or my brother. I had made my decision that I would not take him out after my experiences of bringing him to day care and giving him lifts to town. The matron went on to say that if he wanted to make up his own rules, he would have to leave.

My father was by this time, flustered and demanding to have his say. He denied he was drunk, out late or had been found in a house in the town. I listened to him speaking so authoritatively that if I didn't know the truth, I would have believed him for he sounded so truthful and sincere. He asked what everyone was getting so upset about? Surely at this stage of his life he was entitled to go out for a drink with his friend and that's all there was to it. I thought, this is what I have heard all my life. He was trying to shift the blame for his own actions onto others, something he was very good at. Nothing had changed, he was still living in denial. The matron went on to say that he would not be kept if he continued to break the rules and he said he was not happy about this. He was getting more agitated by the minute, and said he had things to do and he quickly left the office.

Chapter Twenty

Getting His Own Way

My father had never followed any rules in his life. All through his life he had done what he wanted to do. He had bullied, manipulated, verbally and physically abused his family to get his needs met, to live the life he wanted. He never considered what effect his behaviour was having on those around him, so why was he going to bother now? He had used his charm and wit to con people all his life. I often wondered if he had never drank would he have been like this? Or did drink have such a control over him and his mind that it was the only way he could survive in this world?

One day while I was at work my father arrived in with a lady I knew who was a neighbour from near my father's home. He had been drinking and his eyes were red and bloodshot. I spoke with the lady and told her he did not have permission to be out, only with my brother or myself. He told her he had asked for permission then rang her to collect him. My father never came to my place of work before and I wondered was he trying to make a point. Letting me know that he would do what he wanted and no one could stop him. She agreed to drop him straight back to the nursing home in case of any trouble. I'm sure she thought we were all being so horrible and mean, not to allow him out when he wanted to go, but she didn't know the full story.

A week later I met a friend who knew of the problems we were having with my father in the home. She told me that she had seen him at a funeral a few days before and he was on his own for the whole day. He was drinking heavily at the bar in the hotel where the mourners had gathered. This worried me. I rang Michael and told him about it but he knew our father was at the funeral. He brought him out of the nursing home in the morning, let a neighbour drop him off at the funeral and then collected him later that evening from the hotel and took him back to the nursing home. I was angry. The matron had made it clear that he was only to be out with us, she didn't want him left on his own to drink as he would only return to the home in a drunken state for her staff to deal with staff and patient safety was also an issue.

I told Michael this could not be allowed to happen again. If he was prepared to take our father out, he should look after him and try and keep him away from the risk of getting thrown out of the home. We had to do our bit too and support the nursing home to look after him.

On my next visit to the home I asked a nurse how my father had been able to come down to my work with a neighbour? When she checked the notes for the day it was written that he was going out with his daughter and he had signed it. He had lied yet again, soft-talked a nurse and got his way. I told the nurse that day that I would not be taking him out because of his behaviour. She understood and wrote it in the notes.

I visited the home most weeks. Often times my father wasn't there but I didn't enquire where he was. I had done my best to get him looked after and if he was still breaking the rules, there was little I could do about it. Except pray to God he wouldn't be sent home again and he would be kept safe. My uncles were happy and settled and it was such an ease and pleasure to see this. They had respect and dignity in their old age and enjoyed the chat and banter with the nurses.

I had very little contact from Michael, my phone calls and texts were often not answered. I felt helpless to do anything as he seemed to be trying hard to cut us both from his life. On one occasion we were going away on a holiday. I tried contacting him several times to get him to keep an eye on our house while we were away. Phone calls and texts were not answered or replied to.

We went on our holiday and on our return, I wondered what would be the best way forward to connect with him and avoid an argument. It was his birthday the following week so I put a card in the post to him with a little message asking him if he had changed his phone numbers? He rang the next day when he got the card and said he had not changed his numbers. I told him he must have seen the missed calls and texts from my number. He said he had seen them but gave me no explanation why he didn't respond. I felt it was best to leave it and say no more about it, as his behaviour a lot of the time seemed very odd. He was my brother and I didn't want to fall out with him.

Chapter Twenty-one

A COASTAL HOME

My health continued to improve and by 2006, I was feeling a lot better. I still suffered from sinus and ear infections but I was getting stronger.

My herbalist told me I should spend as much time at the sea as possible so my husband and I would head to the coast on our days off. I would sneeze heavily for a few minutes and then my head would clear and I could breathe again through my nose. It was bliss! I would quite happily have stayed sitting on a rock beside the sea breathing the fresh, clean air into my lungs. Having no pressure in my head was a gift, and not having that blocked up sensation all the time was great. I hated returning to the Midlands in the evenings as my head would clog up again.

My husband could see the difference it was making to me. We had sold our shop and made a profit, and we still had our home and farm. Property was booming at the time so it was a good time to sell. It was a very hard decision to make, but both of us felt it was right for us to do.

Our home went on the market and we put a deposit down on a house that was due to be built in the town where I worked. We didn't want to do anything impulsively so we played it safe. Several months later we agreed to sell when we received a firm offer from a neighbour.

His father and the man who left us the farm were very good friends and we were pleased that he was keen to buy it. We knew he would look after it and very soon after, the 'sale agreed' sign went up.

A few days later my brother rang saying he would buy it. I told him it had been sold and we were not going to break an agreement. I wondered why he hadn't expressed an interest in buying it previously, as it had been for sale for months. I wondered where he would get the money from.

I spoke with my uncles and told them we were selling. They didn't say very much but I know they didn't really approve. In their era, land was valuable and not to be parted with. The closing date was set we were on the move. The house we had bought wasn't even started, so when the development fell through, we received our deposit back.

One day we decided to go to the sea. My head was badly blocked up and my ear was burning with the infection. We thought the best decision for my health would be to move away from the Midlands and move to the coast.

I got such relief at the coast that I wished I could just sit on the rocks every day. I could breathe through my nose, the pressure in my head would ease and my ear would settle down. The tightness and wheeze in my chest would go and it felt good. If I lived here all the time, what a life I could have. To be strong and healthy - what I would give for that. Maybe all the stress I was under was affecting me too.

I was concerned though at how we could leave a place we lived in for so long, leave the people, my husband's family and our friends and go to a place where we knew nobody? It was a huge decision.

As the time drew closer to our moving date our decision was made. We would move to the coast. My health was paramount. After all we could build a home again, we could make new friends, and our family and friends from the Midlands could come and visit and enjoy a holiday themselves. I prayed to God for guidance and wisdom for us to go to the right place.

We started our property search on the south-east coast. Property prices had soared and we wanted to tread carefully. We had to make the best decision for us. We settled on a little cottage with a large garden overlooking a bay. It was beautiful. We knew we could get planning permission to build an extension with a view overlooking the bay.

The early days were hard. I remember sitting in the cottage one night with our dogs. My husband had gone to visit his brother. I was alone not knowing anyone, and for a minute, a thought occurred to me. My God what have we done? What is lying ahead for us?

Father strikes again...
I went back to visit the nursing home a few times a month as I did not want my uncles to think I had left them. My father however didn't seem to care one way or another if he saw me or not. I used to contact my brother on my visits to meet him, but he would not get back to me. My father was out and about a lot every day and as I heard no complaints, I thought all was well. I was content on those visits as I was able to connect with my friends. I was starting to feel a lot better, so I knew I had to work on settling in and moving on.

One day in July 2007, a phone call came from the nursing home to say my uncle was being sent to the hospital. They were unable to contact my brother to go with him. I agreed to travel up the next day to be with him. I was determined that I would do my best for my uncles, as despite everything that had happened in the past, I had spent my childhood years living under their roof, and I was always grateful for that. They were victims of a very difficult situation too, I was not alone in that.

I arrived at the nursing home early in the morning. A nurse that I knew told me that when I returned from the hospital with my uncle, the director of nursing wanted to see me. I knew this was not good news. I had always spoken with the matron or nurses about my father's problems. My uncles never caused a problem; I never once received any complaints about them.

I returned from the hospital with my uncle, wondering what was facing me. I said my goodbyes to him and went to see the nurse. She made a phone call and told me to go to the front office.

When I entered the office the boss arose from his seat behind the desk and shook my hand. Beside him stood the nurse who was head of the unit my father was in. The man apologised for what he had to say. I stayed silent and listened. He told me that my father's behaviour was totally unacceptable. He said he was making up his own rules and treating the place like a hotel. My father was constantly drinking and showing no regard for staff or patients and would leave the home when he wanted. The staff had given him several verbal warnings but it made no difference. Because of his behaviour, they could no longer be responsible for him, he was a liability. The nurse told me it was more than her job was worth to keep him on her unit. She was worried about the safety of the other patients, and worried about him causing an accident. Bottom line was - they wanted my father out.

I sat in the chair, shaking. This was the news I dreaded. What would become of my father? He had to be kept safe. He would not seek help for his problem, but how could I, as his daughter leave him with no care? I could understand how this had come about. If he wasn't my father, would I have stayed around him so long? The answer is no. I could understand why they needed him to leave. He wasn't ill - he was an alcoholic. I think they put up with him for such a long time as he was a charmer and very persuasive.

They talked about sending him home. I pleaded my case with them, not to let this happen. I knew if he went home he would be on the road again at night, drinking heavily every chance he could get, and destroying my brother's life. Then my brother would be on to me to sort out the problem, and the cycle would start all over again. I could not fix him; it was up to him to fix himself.

I thanked them for all they had done. I understood that they had made their decision. I drove home that day and prayed my father would not be sent home again.

On my next visit to the nursing home, one of the nurses told me that my father was leaving. She went on to say I should meet with my brother to discuss what was best for his future. I rang my brother and he told me our father was being moved out, because someone more important in the community needed the bed.

I explained to him it was our father's behaviour that was causing him to be moved but my brother would not accept this. He refused to meet me to discuss his future, and went on to say the authorities were allowing him to go to another nursing home. Thank God for that!

At least he wouldn't be let home. I suggested a home outside of a town would be the best option as our father would not have easy access to buying alcohol. A friend phoned me a few days later to tell me she heard that another man had been moved out of the home too, along with my father. Turned out they were drinking buddies. The Health Board's letter read that my father's medical needs didn't merit him being in that nursing home any more, but that they would fund him in a nursing home of his choice. Very clever, I thought, to word a letter in that manner. Not a word in it about his behaviour or alcohol problem.

The days passed and I heard no more. On my next visit to the home my uncle told me my father was going to a nursing home ten miles away. It was in a small village with a shop and lots of pubs. I didn't think it was suitable, but as I was not included in the decision I could only hope that it would work out. I felt nothing would change. My father would move there, make up his own rules again and obtain easy access to pubs.

Chapter Twenty-two

LIFE WAS GOOD

I didn't visit my father in the new home for a few months. He was always short-tempered and cutting with me so I felt it was best not to visit him for a while. I know he probably blamed me for getting him thrown out of the home he had been in.

Months went by and all was quiet. I didn't receive any complaints about my father's behaviour and I wondered if he had changed his ways? Maybe a miracle had happened? Maybe he had learned a lesson? I did make contact with my brother when I was travelling up to meet with him but he still refused to come with me.

I was settling into my new life. My health was better and I joined a papercraft class. I loved the class, and I made some friends, life was good. I applied for a job in a hardware and giftware shop and I got a part-time position which was ideal as it gave me time to do other things. I loved papercraft and once I learned the basics I started to make lots of greeting cards, spending hours on my new hobby. I was then able to sell the cards I made so that was an added bonus.

Bad neighbours...
Our goal to extend our cottage had hit problems. We were granted planning permission without an issue but three weeks before our building work was due to commence, my husband went to see our neighbour. We were new to the area and I felt it would be good to make contact with him and discuss plans on the entrance.

His gateway was beside ours but we had to make a wider entrance to allow access for a car.

Even though we had full planning permission during the conversation our neighbour made it very clear that he was not happy about us doing this. He got quite nasty and swore at us. He said he was giving his house to his son and that we would have to talk to him. My husband rang his son one evening and was on the receiving end of an angry tirade. We were shocked.

We had only just moved to a new town, were granted full planning permission, yet our nearest neighbour clearly was against us. Was that a battle we needed in our life? A rock was thrown through my car window one night when it was parked on the road outside the house. We had a chat about what we could do without getting into legal wrangles with our neighbour and felt it was best to sell up and move away. It was not a good start. Had we gone ahead and built we may never have had peace living there. Our dream was shattered. The plan for the cottage was ideal, but we felt in our hearts it was best to move on.

We then moved to a new house in the town with a view of the sea. We kept a vision that one day we would build our own home as we had done many years ago, but now we had the added bonus of the knowledge and experience from having our own business. We settled down and started making plans for the house that we would build.

Same old problems...
One day while I was busy in my office making cards I received a phone call, it was from the nursing home. My father had fallen and needed quite a few stitches in his head. I made the journey to see him, it was my first visit there. I introduced myself to the nurse when she opened the door to me. She showed me to a room and told me she would let the matron know I had arrived. After a few minutes the matron came in, clearly worried. She introduced herself and shook my hand. Maybe she thought the reason for my

visit was to tell her off over my father's fall and to lay the blame firmly with her. She went on to tell me that my father's drinking was causing major problems in the home. I was not surprised by this.

She went on to say that while drunk, my father had fallen in his room and hit his head on the radiator. It was a miracle he was still alive. He had to be sent to hospital for stitches but was okay. She spoke of the fact that, thank God, he was okay because if the fall had of killed him that night, there would have been serious questions asked about how he was allowed to drink so much in the care of a nursing home. She said she had many battles with my father over his drinking and confiscated whiskey bottles which his visitors had brought him. She would lock his drink away and give him a glass at bedtime. No matter what steps she took, he was still drinking heavily. He was not paying his portion of his pension to the home either, so it meant he had plenty of money. It was the same story yet again. My father was making his own rules. I rang my brother and told him that we both needed to talk to our father about his behaviour and to make sure he was paying the home the correct amount from his pension. My brother was not interested.

I drove home that evening thanking God I lived miles away now. With no support I could not get my father to pay his share. I knew from dealing with him in the past it was his way or no way, and I would only end up upsetting myself in the process. He had to sort out his own life, the issues were his. I felt sorry for the matron that day because I understood everything she said and explained that I knew about the problem. I told her I would do everything I could, but because my brother was avoiding me, it would not be easy. I wondered if my father would be moved on again.

Chapter Twenty-three

A SAD TURN OF EVENTS

After settling into our new home on a weekend visit to the Midlands to stay with friends I had a very strong feeling that I should call to see my uncles as soon as I reached the town. Usually when I went for the weekend I would travel up on the Friday evening and visit the nursing home on the Saturday. But on this occasion, I felt I should drop in first. My uncles were getting ready for bed when I arrived. I didn't stay very long as they were tired. On my way out a nurse stopped me and said they were very worried about my older uncle. He just wasn't himself, she said that he was off his food a bit and just out of sorts. I had noticed that when I visited him, he became a bit agitated, but I put it down to his keenness to get to bed that night.

I left the home that evening and went to stay with friends thinking I would drop in again before the weekend was over. Next day I went to a town nearby to do a few hours work on a stall for a charity I was involved with. It was a busy day and it went quickly.

An hour before we were due to finish, my phone rang. It was the nursing home. I knew it was not good news when the voice asked if I had someone with me. He went on to say that my uncle James, had just collapsed and died. Thank God I went to see him the night before. I left and headed back to the nursing home. I was distraught.

When I arrived at the nursing home, my father was sitting in the corridor with my cousin, they were having tea and biscuits. My father didn't seem too upset and was sober which I was very thankful to see. My first thoughts were - who was with my other uncle? Did he even know? I asked my father about it and he quickly told me it was none of my business.

My father went on chatting to the staff in the home, acting normally. The night was closing in and it was getting late. I felt angry that uncle James had died and the only brother he was really close to was lying in his bed a few rooms away, and didn't know.

I felt had I been able to go and tell him and spend some time with him that evening, it would not have been so much of a shock. As the evening went on, I felt myself getting more upset. My brother could not be contacted so I felt the best thing to do was to leave and return in the morning.

Later that night my brother text me with the funeral details, nothing else. It shook me. My uncle was only gone a few hours and now, arrangements were being made. So quick, so heartless I thought. I lay awake that night shedding tears of sadness and thought of my uncle who was left behind. Did he know of his brother's passing? I thought he would probably not be told until the morning as it was very late when I left the home. They would probably let him have his night's sleep and tell him in the morning.

Next morning, I was up early and had breakfast. I prayed to God to give me strength to face the day. I went to the home and walked the long corridor to my uncle's room. I opened the door. Behind a screen lay his frail frame. He put out his hand to me and tears welled in his eyes, his best friend was gone. I sat with him for a few hours; he spoke about his brother and I just listened. They had spent their whole life together, supported each other and now my uncle was alone. My father was alive but really wasn't bothered about anyone. He lived life for himself. He put on a public show for appearance's sake, but that was it. So long as he had his whiskey and life the way he wanted, everything else was irrelevant.

I spoke to a nurse who told me my brother had arrived at the nursing home very late the night before. She went on to say my father and brother had taken my uncle down to the room where his brother's remains were laid out. Then my uncle was taken back to his room a while later on his own. I was stunned. How could my brother be so cold and heartless, just to tell my uncle of his brother's passing and then just walk away and leave him on his own? The nurse did not seem impressed either. Was I surprised by this behaviour? I suppose not really. I never once saw an ounce of compassion from those men and this day was no different.

Goodbye uncle James...

My uncle's funeral went ahead, all arranged by my brother and father. The evening of the removal from the funeral home was very difficult. My brother had asked a neighbour to look after my uncle David and he arrived to the funeral home in a wheelchair. A group gathered around my uncle's coffin to carry it out to the hearse, and as I stood back I wondered why my husband had been cut off. He had always got on very well with my uncle and most of the people carrying the coffin had no connection with my uncle at all. What was going on? For the sake of peace I said nothing. It was important for me to be able to pay respects to my uncle, and if my brother and father were cutting us off, that was their issue, not ours. Clergy were drafted in for the service. I wondered what my uncle would have thought of this big public show.

He hadn't attended church for many years. The last time he was in a church was at our wedding years before. The day of the funeral I walked beside my father to the grave. On the other side, was a neighbour.

My father was busy chatting away to her and ignored me. He had been drinking - I could smell it on his breath. I prayed to God to give me strength to get through the day. I went back to the pub after the funeral where snacks were served and met with a few friends. I was not only upset because my uncle had just died, but upset at being treated like a stranger by my so-called family.

I thanked God that day for taking me away from that place and giving me the opportunity of a new life.

I left that evening and headed back home. I could have gone and demanded an explanation from my brother but I knew there was little point. Why had he cut me out as if I didn't exist? He had proved to me enough times he was heartless and I knew I would only upset myself even more. Could I as a daughter and a sister really expect any different behaviour from my family?

My father beckoned me over to him as we were leaving. He was sitting at the bar drinking. I left feeling very hurt, that he only wanted to acknowledge me when he was drunk. I didn't go over to him as drunken words meant nothing to me. We left after saying our goodbyes to friends.

I returned to the nursing home a few days later. My uncle David was very lonely after his brother died. I decided not to visit my father. He had treated me like a stranger at the funeral and I felt it best to stay away from him for the time being.

A month later I visited the home again. Over the years I had got to know the staff very well and they knew of the difficult family situation. A nurse stopped me in the corridor and asked me how I was and if I knew about the acknowledgement card that had been printed for my uncle James? I told her I didn't know about it, she then told me my name was not on it. She went on to say that the nurses in the home were disgusted as they knew the input I had with my uncle's care. She said she would give me the card when she was finished her rounds - I told her I would be in uncle David's room.

Later she came into the room with a white envelope in her hand, she put it into my handbag and told me not to open it until I got home. I spent some time with my uncle and told him I would be back the next day.

Excluded once again...

I walked out the door wondering what was written in the card in my bag. I was confused as to why I didn't get a card in the post. I sat in the car and with trembling hands, I opened the envelope. The card had a photo of my uncle as a very young man. As I read down through the words, my eyes filled with tears. The nurse was right; my name was omitted. My father, uncle and my brother's names were on it. That was it. I was heartbroken. I spent my childhood in this man's home. I had looked after him over the years and had done all I could for him. I'd been a big part of his life. I had been cut out of the funeral and my name omitted from his memorial card.

I went to my friend's house that evening. When I walked into her kitchen she was sitting at the table. She asked me if I got on okay; I said nothing and just placed the card on the table in front of her. She couldn't believe her eyes. She knew of my constant visits to my uncle and my role in his life.

I returned to see my uncle the next day and on the way back I passed my childhood home. It had a five-bar metal farm gate across the driveway which was always closed whenever I drove past. The big Georgian house which was partially hidden behind trees looked dreary. There were no lights on and no warmth about it whatsoever. I wondered what state the house was now in, as nothing had been done to it for so long.

My health was so much better now and I was thankful. I even thought if I hadn't suffered sinus and health issues, we would have never moved away, so maybe those issues were a blessing in disguise. I'd been forced to move to a new place away from all the nastiness and dysfunction. I could never change my family, I could only ever change myself and be responsible for my own actions. Their actions were their problem - how I reacted to those actions was my issue. I felt hurt over what had happened but felt I had always done my best. I didn't want to grow bitter so I prayed to God to give me the grace to always do and say the right thing even in the most difficult of circumstances - and to forgive the family that had and continued to hurt me so much

Chapter Twenty-four

Executor Issues

One day a letter arrived from my brother which stated that my uncle had made a will dividing his assets between us and we were both executors. He went on to say that, thank God, he had encouraged our uncle to make a will the year before, because no one else had a claim now. He added my uncle's assets were nil but he was due back a payment from the nursing home for overcharging and this would pay for the funeral. It closed with a statement that if I did get anything from this payment, I was to return it to my uncle's relatives. I reread the letter in disbelief.

As I was an executor on the will I had questions. My uncle was in a nursing home with a surplus going into his account every week. He wasn't a smoker or a drinker and his everyday needs were met by the nursing home, so how could the account be nil? I had given his pension book into the home to look after and had given my brother €3,000 of my uncle's money not long before. Where had his money gone? Questions had to be answered. I went to see the lady in the office at the nursing home who was dealing with patients' accounts and told her my story.

She told me my brother had removed my uncle's pension book a year before and taken most of the money out of his account. My brother would bring my uncle down to the office and get him to sign the necessary paperwork. The lady told me there should be plenty of money to pay for his funeral before the nursing home payment came back. She went on to say I should seek legal advice on the matter.

I left her office that day feeling very confused. As executor, I had a duty to my uncle to see that everything was in order and his wishes were carried out. I could not overlook the fact that money was unaccounted for, and my brother clearly did not want me to benefit in any way from my uncle. I went to see a solicitor to find out what I should do. He read my brother's letter and agreed it was clear that my brother didn't want me to receive anything. He went on to say that as an executor on the will I had a duty of care to my uncle, and to protect myself from being involved in the issue of his finances, I had two choices - if my brother refused to discuss my uncle's affairs, I could take the case to court - or I could pull out as executor. I left the office to consider the options.

All my own fault...
I tried to contact my brother but he would not answer his phone or reply to my messages. I then wrote to him asking him to meet up to discuss the matter. I also asked him in the letter to explain the reason for excluding me from my uncle's acknowledgement card. He replied and told me there was nothing to discuss - that it was sorted and that it was my own fault.

I was not included in the card. He went on to say our father needed money too. I decided to meet with the solicitor who drew up my uncle's will. He was also my brother's solicitor. He told me my brother had opened a joint account with my uncle a year before, in the credit union, and as it was a joint account, my brother did not have to disclose the details. I was taken back to discover the dates that my brother had removed my uncle's money from the nursing home and opened the joint credit union account, was very soon after the date of the will. I wondered had my brother very cleverly put a plan in place to make sure he would be the only beneficiary of my uncle's account.

I made a decision to pull out as executor on the grounds that I could not get any information about my uncle's financial affairs. I felt it was the best decision, as I did not want to drive my brother further away and felt my uncle would not have approved of legal action. It was a difficult decision and may look as if I didn't want to fight for my entitlements. I had deep concerns about my brother's mental health as his behaviour was odd and I felt it was best to walk away and protect myself. If my brother wanted to grab everything, that was his issue not mine. I would be okay.

One day I visited the nursing home and met a nurse who knew a little of the history in my family. She'd attended my uncle's funeral and she told me her heart went out to me that day. She said she understood how I felt. Tears streamed down my face. She was telling the truth. My uncle had allowed me to live under his roof as a child. If not for him I would have ended up in a care home. She hugged me and told me to take care of myself. I thanked her and walked away.

That day I met my father outside the main door smoking a cigarette. He had been drinking. His eyes were bloodshot and his speech was slurred. I told him I had received a letter from my brother, I then asked him if he knew what went on with my uncle's affairs and where all his money had gone. His voice changed, he was not happy. He swore at me and told me never to come back.

Chapter Twenty-five

TOTAL DEPENDENCE

Uncle David's health was going downhill. I wondered if he was losing his will to live since his brother had passed away. Every time I visited, I could detect a difference. He was sad and lonely. My husband went to see the cleric who organised my uncle's funeral to explain to her how I had played a big part in his life and how I had been ignored at the funeral. She listened but made no comment.

I visited my father's nursing home a few months later. As I approached the reception desk I could hear my father shouting. I stood behind him where he could not see me. He was drunk and was shouting at one of the nurses, demanding his whiskey. I felt sorry for the staff having to deal with this. They were fighting a losing battle with him. He would do as he always did - if he wanted to drink he would, and no one would stop him.

He staggered down the corridor away from where I was standing to his room. When he was out of sight I went and spoke to the nurse. She told me of the constant battles she was having with him over his drinking. He would not listen. I waited a few minutes before I went to his room. I brought a friend with me that day as I knew if I had someone with me, he would be on his best behaviour. We approached his room. I wondered what we would meet. Would he be angry he didn't get his way or would I be swore at? Anything was possible. I opened the door and found him sitting beside the bed with a half-filled glass of whiskey in his hand, he was very drunk. He greeted us both, and started to cry. He went on to say in a drunken voice that he was very lonely. It broke my heart - in front of me sat a man who could have been anything he wanted to be. He was clever and intelligent, and had been given a good start in life by his father. He had married, and had two children but he'd lost so much, all because of his love for alcohol. I was now looking at a sad, lonely old man destroyed by the life choices he made. He was my father, someone I should have been proud of, but that day I thanked God I didn't follow in his footsteps.

The nursing home had offered him help to get him off the dependency of alcohol, but he denied he was the one with the problem. Maybe he had to bury his pain with alcohol. The abuse of my mother, the way he treated my uncles and now he was turning against me too for no reason. Was this his way of coping? Did he know deep down he was wrong but couldn't admit it to himself? Was his pain too deep?

I spoke to a nurse on my way out and told her how he was treating me and it was too upsetting for me to see him in the state I found him that day. I asked her to let me know if his health was failing and I would return. I needed to take care of myself and with the issues with my brother, it was healthier to stay away. Leaving the nursing home that day I thought back to a conversation I had previously with a man I knew, whose father had been an alcoholic all his life. He had told me that the only time I would have peace in my life was when my father was dead. Harsh words I thought, but so true. My father was never prepared to admit he had a problem that could be helped, so nothing was going to change.

More family problems...

In the following months I received letters from my brother. He point-blank refused to meet me, but one of his letters aroused deep concerns. He spoke of his own funeral and how it would be an army affair. Several lines in the letter went into great detail about the arrangements. I was worried. Where was this coming from, and what could I do? I went to visit a man who I knew had some contact with my brother. I asked him to read the letter and when he did, he looked at me with tears in his eyes. He said he hoped he was not planning on doing something stupid. I told him my brother had totally cut me out of his life and asked him to keep an eye on him. He promised he would.

The months passed and my uncle David was getting weaker. One day I received a phone call from the nursing home to say he was very unwell so I went to visit him. He was very frail and after speaking with the nurse I knew his days were numbered. I decided to stay with a friend for a few days close to the nursing home. He drifted off to sleep many times but seemed glad to see me every time he woke up. We spoke a few words and he didn't appear to be in pain. Late in the evening a nurse came in and said she would sit with him for a while, so I went away and had something to eat and a rest. She told me my brother was coming in later and would stay for the night. I left planning to return early next morning.

I rang early the next morning and asked the nurse would she ask my brother to come and collect me from where I was staying. She agreed. I waited for an hour but there was no sign of him.

I woke my friend and asked her to give me a lift. I hated disturbing her but I was worried about my uncle being left on his own.

When I arrived I went into my uncle's room and found Michael sitting by his bed. I asked him why he had refused to collect me? He never answered and quickly left the room without a word. I was upset but didn't want my uncle to realise this, so I told myself to be strong. I reminded myself that I was there for my uncle and that's what counted.

Over the next two days I sat by his bed. He was slowly slipping away. He got weaker and weaker and was only able to speak in a whisper. He would wake and when he knew I was there he would drift back to sleep again.

A minister came in and prayed over him. I said my own prayer that he would be at peace and not suffer. I asked the Lord to give me strength to face the days ahead and for the courage to stay with him until the end. Friends brought me in sandwiches and dropped in to ensure I was okay. I stayed with my uncle because I knew the end was near. He was not able to take any fluids as his swallow had failed. My father and brother arrived and I could tell my father had been drinking. He tried to give my uncle a drink. I told him he could not take any liquids but my father lifted his head and tried to force him to drink so I called a nurse. My brother stood and watched without a word. The nurse ushered the both of them out, they were gone without a word to me.

Later that day, my cousin arrived and stayed for a while. We both knew my uncle had not long to live. She rang her husband to tell him it was not good, I heard her saying to him that I was with her. He wanted to know what I was doing there, she hung up visually upset by his remarks. She knew this was unfair. I wondered what was going on but I also know the man had recently became very friendly with my brother. Was my brother telling him lies about me?

I would try and visit the nursing home during the week whereas Michael would always visit on Sundays, was this so he could be seen? Where was he when his uncle was dying? Did he contact me to see if I was okay? The answer was no. But then why did that not surprise me? I tried to put all the nasty negative thoughts out of my head to stay strong for my uncle. I would not let him die alone, no matter how hard it was to watch him fade away.

My husband arrived to support me, I was happy to see him. A nurse told us to go out for something to eat and that she would sit with my uncle. She said she would wait on our return before giving him any more morphine. We felt in our hearts that this was going to be his last night with us as he was fading fast.

It was indeed his last night; he passed peacefully in the early hours of the morning. I watched the life drain from his body but I was very thankful I was able to comfort him in his final days of life. He was now at peace.

Goodbye Uncle David…

I wrote a letter to put in his coffin - it was a letter of thanks and of apology for the life he had endured. It was my way of forgiving him for all his nasty behaviour over the years towards me. I had no axe to grind with him. He was a victim of a very bad situation and he had been powerless to change. I wished him rest and peace.

The minister rang me and said she had arranged to meet my brother and father later that afternoon to discuss the funeral details and that I was welcome to come along. I thanked her and said I would. My father and brother were a little startled when I arrived, they seemed very uncomfortable that I was there. I greeted everyone and sat down, the arrangements were made and the minister asked if there was anything I wanted to add? I did state a few ideas and she jotted them down. I was happy that I was being included this time.

The funeral went ahead. Strangers were drafted in again to help. My husband was not asked to carry the coffin and a neighbour ended up looking after my father for the day. As the coffin was carried into the church she stood linking my father's arm. I was angry - this was not her place. She had probably been told by my brother that I would not support him. I waited near the church door. The coffin passed and my father stood behind it with the neighbour by his side. I entered in front of her and offered to link my father up the aisle. She didn't move. I was determined to take my rightful place beside my father and she had no right to interfere. I walked him up the aisle, I saw my brother sitting in a seat opposite on his own. As the funeral progressed I realised that nothing I had requested was done and this was puzzling.

After the funeral, the minister explained to my husband that my brother had asked her not to fulfil my wishes. I was angry. Why didn't he have the decency to contact me himself instead of going behind my back?

I started to think of the days ahead, living beside the sea in my happy home. I focused on the good in my life and the blessings

God had given me. A few more hours and I would be free. I had done all I could for my uncle and was grateful that I was with him in his final days, as I didn't want him to die alone. A funeral was only a day and no matter how badly my brother and father were shunning me, it was their problem, not mine. I had always done my best, and nothing would pull me down. I knew the truth - that I was being excluded because of guilt and shame.

After the burial everyone gathered in the pub. I spoke with friends and saw my father heading to the bar and taking a seat. People were buying him whiskey and he was happy. I watched him from a distance waving his hands around, getting his point across to those who wanted to listen. When people got up to leave, I said goodbye to my friends. On my way out I stopped near the place where my father sat to say goodbye to a friend. I could see my father out of the corner of my eye waving his hand, trying to get my attention. His eyes were bloodshot and he was drunk. I turned away from him, I was going home.

He had hurt me enough, he had depended on a neighbour to be by his side for the funeral, he had treated me like a stranger and then in his drunken state, he wanted to talk to me before I left? I knew what it would be - words that meant nothing - words that would hurt me again.

Was history repeating itself? When my mother was alive she took the blame and now the buck was being passed to me. But thank God I had a good life away from the toxic family I grew up in. I left that day sad because both of my uncles were gone, but realised I had done my best for them. I drove back home.

Chapter Twenty-six

LOVE AND RESPECT IS PRICELESS

A few weeks later I went back to visit my father. He was ageing and I felt I should make an effort to see him. During my visit Michael also arrived to see him. I remained calm and had a chat with him, inviting him for a coffee to try and make amends before I returned home the following day but he said no. My father then spoke and said there was no need for talking to revisit the past. He said everything had been sorted. I said nothing but in my heart I knew he was right - that he was involved too in spending my uncle's money before he died.

I left that day feeling it was best not to return for a while. My brother had severed his ties with me, having treated me so badly, my father had done the same. I felt I needed to take time out and look after myself. I had done all I could and felt getting on with my life was the best thing I could do.

I had my own life - there but by the grace of God go I. I was thankful I wasn't like them. They may be my family but I was a totally different person to them. I didn't need their toxic attitudes pulling me down. I knew if my father was ill, the nursing home would contact me and let me know, but now I had to protect myself.

I got on with work and life. We found a site and decided we would build our dream home. Life was good, work was busy and I did some crafting in my spare time. I was also feeling more settled, having made friends in the area.

I was still taking medication prescribed by the herbalist and was feeling so much better. My head was clear and I could taste my food again. My ear problem had cleared up and having proper ear wax was a real treat. My chest was clear and I was able to get out and enjoy the sea air and a walk on the beach with my husband and dogs. For the first time in a long time, I felt healthy.

I knew however my feet were not good, I was on my feet a lot in work and one foot in particular started to give me a lot of pain. I had always worn flat, wide shoes and orthotics since I was old enough to look after my feet, but I knew because of the mistreatment my feet underwent in my youth, time was probably catching up.

One day I had a phone call from the nursing home. My father had taken a mild turn. The nurse told me he was very ill and his health was going downhill fast, I said I would visit him. She recommended that I shouldn't come on my own as she knew he could be very abusive. She offered to come with me if I wanted to see him. I was happy with this as I knew he would be on his best behaviour if I had someone else there, so I went to visit him the next day.

It had been a few months since I had visited and I noticed he had failed a lot. Drink, cigarettes and age were taking a toll on his body. He looked up when we entered the room. He was sitting with another resident, a lady, and they were both smoking. I greeted him and she asked who I was and where I was from? I could tell by his expression, he was angry, his mood changed in an instant. He told the lady to mind her own business and not to be asking questions, then he got up from his chair and left the room.

I stood with the nurse beside me, shaken by his actions. I could smell whiskey from him when he passed by. I wondered what was going on with him. The man who I used to be afraid of in his drunken rages was now old, frail and very angry. Was he angry because I walked in on him without warning? I look like my mother and I wondered in his frailty was it her he saw standing in front of him and that his shame and guilt was coming back to haunt him. He went to his room and I left for home. I felt it was best to leave him alone, so I left.

Gone for good...
A week later I went to a Bible study at a friend's house, afterwards I lifted my phone out of my bag to switch it off silent mode. I was shocked when I looked at the screen, I had sixteen missed calls, so I knew something was wrong. Before I had time to check who the calls were from, my husband was at the door. I went out to meet him and he told me that my father had collapsed and died suddenly. Tears filled my eyes - I was in shock. My father was dead and my last visit to see him had not been a good one. I couldn't believe he was gone.

I went back home that evening and rang my brother. I said I would be up the following day to help arrange the funeral. Later that night I received a call from a close friend who went to the nursing home when she heard my father had died. She knew my history of how I had been cast adrift when my uncles died and she knew how it had upset me. She said that a few of my brother's and father's friends were at the home. They along with my brother were organising the funeral between them and my name was not mentioned. Upon hearing this, I felt it was best if I didn't meet with my brother the next day. I rang the minister and told her I would not be up but would like to contribute to the service by picking a hymn. She said she would ring me back. I also text my brother but I didn't get a reply. I felt I had to keep my strength up to get through the funeral and that it was best to stay away. The next day passed and I heard nothing about the funeral. The following morning I went to the petrol station to check the papers to see if any arrangements were published. I opened the Irish Independent and there it was, his funeral notice. I couldn't believe my brother did not tell me.

Later that night the minister rang me and said everything was sorted and if I wanted I could add a prayer. I was cross with her, but I said nothing. I felt hurt that she had not allowed me to pick a hymn as I requested, but even if I did, my brother would probably have changed it anyway.

The following days were difficult. I had the support of my husband and friends so I knew I would be okay. I sat in the funeral home with a friend on one side and my husband on the other. My brother stayed right beside the coffin, away from where we sat. A man came over and asked my husband to carry the coffin. Why was he asking? Why could my cousin who seemed to be the main organiser, not ask himself? He and my brother had become firm friends since my uncles died. He was the one who claimed I was never there, and that I did nothing for my uncles.

Before I left the funeral, I made my way over to my brother and asked if we could meet for a chat. He just stood behind a woman he was talking to and ignored me. I had tears in my eyes and told him I was going home. How could he see his sister upset like that and not even speak to me? I knew in my heart he was refusing to meet me as he knew he had wronged me over many things and had no excuse for his actions.

I had tried my best with Michael and had always helped him out when I could. Even when I worked in the furniture shop, I purchased a mattress for his bed as the one he was sleeping on was in tatters.

I could not make any sense of him. Was it greed or the influence my father had on him? I had seen the heartless side of him so many times over the years, so his reaction did not really surprise me. I was expecting something from him that he was unable to give. He was stunted and damaged from his past. It had upset me though that he had obviously been telling lies about me.

A week later a text came to my phone. I knew at that hour in the morning it was probably from my brother. The phone was downstairs in the kitchen so my husband went down and brought it up to me. He saw the message was from my brother and I asked him to read it. My husband appeared shocked.

He said he did not want to repeat the message to me as it was sick. He wanted to delete it off my phone but I thought it was best that I should see it.

I read the message and I felt sick to my stomach. It was gruesome details about how our father had died - how he had collapsed and blood had sprayed from his body, covering the floors, walls and the sink in the room. That the nurses had an awful job cleaning up the room after him.

With these type of texts now arriving I attained a new phone number for my phone. I had to prevent my brother from contacting me in this manner as it was upsetting me all the time. I just had enough.

I went back to the nursing home to thank them for the care they gave my father. It was hard to go back to that home, but I felt I needed to speak to someone about his death. I met with the nurse who was on duty the night my father died. I told her of my brother's text. She went on to explain that my father had collapsed and died moments later. A small amount of blood had come from his nose, but that was it. She was there and saw it all. I wondered what a sick mind my brother had to sent me a text with a totally different story. The staff wished me well and told me to take care of myself. I went to visit the graves, said a little prayer and drove home. I was glad to be able to drive away to my very different life.

A family wedding...
A few months later, a friend rang me to tell me my brother was getting married. He was fifty years old and hadn't many girlfriends that I knew of. Soon after, a wedding invitation came in the post. I suspected it would have looked bad if he did not send us an invitation - maybe his future wife would have questioned him. I sent a card, thanking them for the invitation, wished them well and said we would not be attending.

Had things been normal between us I would have been there to wish them well. It saddened me that the only brother I had was getting married and I felt unable to attend because of his previous behaviour. I knew that by not going to the wedding, people would blame me, but this didn't really bother me as they didn't know the truth. The people who knew me and my story supported me in my decision not to attend. I had been hurt enough. I could always make allowances for my father's behaviour, he was an alcoholic. At least he had an excuse - my brother had none.

After the wedding was over, a friend told me she heard a card had been read out at the reception from us apologising for our absence, that we had another engagement that day. I was livid. If this was true, someone had doctored my card to make me look bad. What other engagement was as important as your brother's wedding? I wondered who done that.

Surgery to correct my painful past...
As the days went by my foot got worse. My podiatrist told me surgery was my only option as new insoles would only help for a short time. My metatarsal bones had dropped down through the fat pad on the ball of my foot and the nerves between my toes were getting caught. The pain was unbearable at times and I found I was only able to walk on the outside part of my foot. This meant I kept spraining my ankle a lot. I dreaded the surgery as I knew it was going to be major. All my metatarsal bones and my big toe had to be broken, straightened and bone removed from two of my toes to get a proper shape on my foot. Metal pins would be placed in my feet to keep the bones straight while they healed. It was going to be a slow recovery but I knew I could not carry on as I was. Walking on my feet was becoming more and more difficult and my other foot was going the same way as well, so I knew I had no choice. It was hard facing the surgery. More pain to face. At the hospital I was nervous but hopeful that the final outcome would allow me to walk free of pain.

The surgery went ahead and a cast was put on my foot. When I came around after the surgery I was extremely sick from the effects of the anaesthetic, I even passed out. After the numbness wore off, the pain kicked in and I was pumped full of painkillers via a tube attached to a vein on the back of my hand. I was weak, unable to eat or sleep very well.

Recovery was a long road. An excess of calcium built up on the bones that were broken, causing me more pain. Six months later, I noticed one of the toes had dropped down and was lying in under the toe next to it. I went back to see the surgeon who told me the ligament had snapped in my toe causing it to drop. The little toe next to it was rising up straight. He said he would need to perform more surgery on the two bones to correct this.

I went ahead with the surgery and the foot was opened again on one side. Pins were placed in the toes to keep them straight while they healed. A few weeks later I was back on my feet again. I still had pain in the foot and my other foot was becoming a lot more painful, I agreed to have a course of injections for some relief. This meant a small improvement, but I was still in a lot of pain and very restricted with driving and walking. My other foot was deteriorating too but I could not go ahead with any more surgery until I had at least one dependable foot.

Work was out of the question. It was a difficult time as I was only experiencing this problem because of neglect of my feet growing up. It brought back the memories of my father's abuse and neglect. I told myself there was no point in being cross or angry about it. He had passed away, he was now gone. Let God be his judge. I had several options. I could be angry, cross, or feel like a victim of a bad situation. Feeling like this would only affect me in a very negative way as well as those around me. It would slowly destroy and eat into me like an acid. I made a choice that I would not let this happen.

In those two years going through my own struggles, I received many blessings. I met many people and friends gathered around and took me places, they even came and cleaned my house when

I was unable. During that time too, I met many people going through worse struggles than me - broken marriages, job losses, depression and severe health problems. I often thought of the phrase: 'I complain I have no shoes, and today I met the man who has no feet.' I felt despite my pain I was in a position to help others.

As time progressed after the surgery I noticed I was not getting any better. I had to use crutches to keep me mobile and driving was a problem. My other foot was becoming really painful and I wondered at times what I was going to do. The following year I decided to take a course of acupuncture. I did not want to resort to painkillers; tablets would have only masked the problem and in the long term would have resulted in other health issues to deal with. After a few sessions I felt a lot better. The pain was easing and my toes were starting to move freely. I noticed another of the toes was starting to rise up and overlap the toe beside it. It didn't cause any extra pain; it was just uncomfortable.

I felt if I was able, I could undergo the surgery on my other foot before the end of the year. I returned to the surgeon and booked in to get the second foot done the following week. It was great to get a swift appointment as it didn't give me a chance to think much about what was ahead. I dreaded facing it again after the last big surgery.

I went to the hospital on the morning of the surgery. My foot was in a lot of pain and I knew without this intervention it would continue to get worse. My other foot was sore but not too severe, and I knew in the next few weeks ahead it would be rested. I met the surgeon outside the theatre. He looked at my other foot with the toe overlapping and said I needed another surgery on it - not news I wanted to hear. I'd already had two surgeries on that foot and now I needed another one. He went on to say that it would get a lot worse and cause a lot of problems in future years if left untreated. I asked him if he could do the whole lot that day? He explained that was not an option as it would leave me unable to walk for a long time.

I had surgery and left the hospital two days later. I could bear weight on my heel, so with the crutches I managed to do what I needed to do. The pain was bearable and when I went back for a check-up, the surgeon told me he performed a percutaneous surgery on my foot this time, which meant I had no big open wounds as in the previous surgeries. After both of these I had infection. This time the risk of infection was a lot lower and hopefully healing would be a lot quicker. After three weeks the wires were removed from my toes and the bandages came off. It would take time for the pain to ease and swelling to go down and the bones to heal. I prayed that I would not have to have any more surgery on that foot.

All this had taught me patience. My timing and God's timing are often two different times. I have learned in my life to trust God in all things. I knew in my childhood a hand of protection was with me. My faith has kept me strong and gives me hope in a new and better tomorrow. Sometimes it's when we are going through the trials of life, we see God at work. He plays His part, but we also have to do ours. Those times when I felt so low, I handed it all over to Him. He created me, He protected me in the family unit I was born into and gave me a courage, strength and understanding to rise up and claim all the good He had for me.

The pain and suffering I have gone through with my feet will move into my past. My life has taught me understanding and care for others and it has moulded me into the person I am today. I am proud of that. I thank God every day for His gift of life. Just like my father had free will and choices to make in his life, so do I. The choices I make every day have the power to influence my future and the future of those around me. I want to reflect the joy and peace in my life that I have been given. Despite the broken world I came into, I have choices that will give me joy and peace; other choices will give me nothing but despair. It is my life and I am responsible for it. With God's grace I will make the right choices.

The world we live in today is crumbling. We have more technology than ever, we can even send men to the moon. Everything is acceptable in our society now and it's easier to blame others for the problems in our lives. Our culture is well-known for its alcohol abuse and the problems it causes. Our hospital and A&E units are full of so-called social drinkers at the weekends. How can it be a fun night out to go out and end up in hospital because of an excess of drink? Men, women and children's lives are destroyed by the acceptable level of alcohol consumption in our country, families are destroyed. If there is a reason to celebrate an occasion or drown our sorrows, it always seems to involve alcohol. People complain they can't go to the pub to socialise because they can't drink and drive. If they go to socialise why not go and have a soft drink? Why does it have to be alcohol when it's such a toxic poison to our system, affecting our brains and bodies. It is beyond my understanding and I know a lot of people would consider me odd and boring because I don't go to the pub. I am very happy in my life and don't need to back up my life with alcohol. If the need arises I will go to the pub and have an Irish coffee on occasion but I am very happy to drink a soft drink.

The suicide rate is rising in our country and we have a major drug problem. Young people are losing their lives every day because they are choosing to put drugs in their systems - it is cool and fashionable to do this. Some drugs are sold as soft drugs but all drugs can kill, or alter the mind.

Why do people start on a path like this? Our drinking culture is made out to be part of normal Irish life - so is the drug culture heading the same way? It breaks my heart to read the papers or hear the news of people dying from drugs or a mixture of drugs and alcohol - the family is left behind to pick up the broken pieces. In some cases, because the family are consuming drink and taking drugs, the children grow up in the home thinking it is normal behaviour.

Society has become so used to hearing about suicides, drug and alcohol-related accidents and deaths that we are becoming immune to it. I can remember people telling me my father was always in great spirits, and what was the harm in him taking a few drinks? They did not know of the devastation those so called few drinks caused in our family.

Chapter Twenty-seven

Final Thoughts

My friends who are aware of my traumatic past have often said I should put my story into words. I have changed my name and my relatives' names to avoid embarrassing my family. I have no contact with my brother now which breaks my heart. I hope this book will help at least one person along life's path. This is my sole purpose for putting my story into words.

I pray it will give hope in a very dark and broken world. Whatever is falling and crumbling around us, we do not have to fall with it. We can rise up and be strong and choose our own road. I do know the best handbook on life is the Bible. The teachings and Scripture give guidelines for the best life God wants for us. If we follow these principles in life, all will be well.

There will be struggles, there will be pain and loss, life will seem very unfair but with God on our side we will never be alone. He is our protector and guide, and He wants the best life for us. He has given us free will to make our own life choices and is beside us when we fall. I wish you peace and hope - the same as I have found, and I wish you well.

If you are a recovering alcoholic, I am delighted you have taken the time to read my story, and maybe it will let you see the pain and suffering your family went through while you were drinking. I wish you well on your journey of recovery.

Alcoholism is a disease and it's one disease that has a cure. If you admit you have the disease that is the first part of the treatment. It is the first step in a long but worthwhile journey. It is the beginning of a cure, and day by day with the right help, you can turn your life around. I often prayed my father would change but by his choice, he never did. He had lots of opportunities, but lived in denial all his life. What a shame, what a waste. His life is over; however, yours is not.

If like me, you were brought up in a dysfunctional alcoholic home, know you are valued and no matter what negative words were spoken, be assured that those words were not true. When you make your own way in the world, you can choose the life you want to have and the people you want to be around. Our future can be good, despite our past. Forgiveness gives you the key of freedom to move on with your life. We can forgive. It takes time and it does not mean we should go back and tolerate abuse; sometimes it's healthy to protect yourself and stay away from people who refuse to respect you. It can be difficult to stand alone and make healthy choices because sometimes that means breaking free from people who pull you into their way of living.

We are blessed with one life on this beautiful earth, life is such a gift. I look at the flowers in the garden and the little birds on the feeder. The world we live in is filled with beautiful things for us to enjoy. Step by step, life can get better. No matter what difficult situation you are in, there is always hope that you will get the opportunity to change it for the better. It takes strength and courage, and with God's help and guidance, it can happen. You were created by God, and He is there for you and for me. We just have to ask Him to be part of our lives. He loves us and wants the very best for us. He does His part and we have to do ours.

Be kind to yourself and give yourself all the time you need. For me I love to cook for ourselves and for others. I love to share the gifts and knowledge I have with others, I am living the life that I love and want. I thank God every day for the wisdom and strength to carry on, no matter what each day brings.

Not all my friends have the same beliefs as I have but I don't judge them. People are not perfect and never will I be. We all make mistakes and do things we shouldn't - we are human after all. Forgiveness is wonderful. It's hard to do sometimes, but it frees us from all bitterness and anger. Forgiving the past will make a better tomorrow.

We can't choose the family we are born into. We don't have a say about our height or the colour of our hair. We do however, have the power to make good or bad decisions.

The life my mother had often saddens me. I know it was beyond my control to help her, and now I am so thankful I know the truth about why she was not part of my childhood. I am so thankful for the people I met in a timely fashion. My mother's life was destroyed by the effects of my father's drinking; her life was a living nightmare of pain and abuse.

Never underestimate the pain of mental abuse. The constant put downs, nasty comments and lack of respect have the power to destroy a person. It is hidden and leaves no scars on the body, only in the mind. It destroys self-esteem, self-belief and confidence – three elements so important in living a good life.

Our childhood is the founding years of our lives. We are like sponges and absorb all the information given to us. We believe and trust our caregivers. After all, they are our family, so we should be able to depend on them. Growing up, my belief was that everyone had a family like mine. It was only when I became an adult I saw that a normal family should be a loving, caring unit, not a place of struggle, neglect and pain.

Over the years my brother always had our front gates painted white. I always thought it was ironic how the place always appeared outwardly so perfect, but inside was crumbling and rotting with the abuse and pain.

Today the house is slowly crumbling due to neglect. Holes are appearing in the roof and slates are dropping to the ground, one by one. The fence is shabby, the paint is peeling off. All that remains are clumps of daffodils in the front lawn and driveway, some planted by me and some planted probably by my grandparents.

I wonder what the inside of the house is like now. With the holes in the roof, I reckon the timbers and floorboards must be rotting fast. I wonder what became of all the antiques and furniture in the house and my parents' wedding presents. Many days I dusted the furniture and ornaments in the sitting room. The fancy glass oil lamps and pieces of Wedgwood were all dusted. I often thought it was a pointless exercise, spending hours cleaning them because I'd return a week later and the dust would have reappeared. Today if the valuables are still in the house, they must be coated in a thick layer of dust. Maybe they have been taken to my brother's new house or were sold off for a tidy profit.

Some people have said to me, it was shameful to witness such a fine property left to battle the elements. I can fully understand this outside point of view. The house looks like the beautiful Georgian property it is, with a long winding avenue surrounded by trees and if restored to its original state, it would make a beautiful home.

My brother, and his wife and child now live in a house nearby. I often think of the child - I hope and pray he will be okay. I am not part of his life as I have never met him. I hope he will grow up with an open mind. I am thankful I know the truth about my mother and not what my father wanted me to believe. He accused her of being useless and uncaring toward her children, maybe history has repeated itself with my nephew? Time will tell.

Through these pages I have spoken of the sadness but also of the happiness. I have learned valuable lessons and I write as a survivor, not as a victim. Today I still suffer with pain in my feet and I can't do all the things I would like. I started a care course last year, but had to leave it as the pain became too severe through the winter months, my sinus problem also returned. I just take each day as it comes, and with God's help, all will be well.

Final Thoughts

I do some volunteer work with my craft classes when I can. The people I encounter, share their situations with me. I listen to their stories which are filled with pain and I have an understanding, because I have been there. I can appreciate their pain and I try to encourage them with hope. Maybe this is where I should be now? I am happy - totally at peace and have forgiven my past. I believe truth comes out in its own time - and this is the time to write this book.

I write in tribute to my mother and look forward to the day I will meet her again. We will have a lot to talk about.

To you the reader, I thank you for taking the time to read this book. I wish you well on your life journey. Whatever part of the path you are on, I wish you strength and God's blessings to face the future. Trust all will be well, make good choices and be the best you can be.

To the people who have been there for me, I thank you all, for whatever part you have played. The choices we make today will have an impact on our tomorrows.

For more information or to contact the author visit

www.WhenAFatherLeaves.com

www.ingramcontent.com/pod-product-compliance
Lightning Source LLC
Chambersburg PA
CBHW052131010526
44113CB00034B/1621